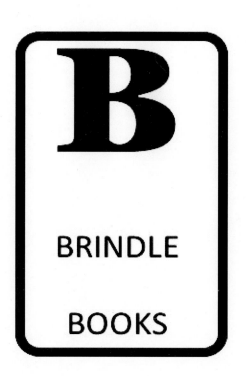

BRINDLE

BOOKS

https://www.brindlebooks.co.uk

The Grassington Murder :

The Story of the Infamous Tom Lee

by

Mark Bridgeman

CONTENTS

THE
TYBURN CHRONICLE,
OR,
VILLAINY DISPLAY'D
IN ALL ITS BRANCHES.

CONTAINING

An AUTHENTIC ACCOUNT
OF THE
LIVES, ADVENTURES, TRYALS, EXECUTIONS,
and LAST DYING SPEECHES of the
MOST NOTORIOUS MALEFACTORS

Of all Denominations, who have suffered for

Bigamy,	Murders,	Riots,
Forgeries,	Perjury,	Sodomy,
Highway-Robberies,	Piracy,	Starving,
House-breaking,	Rapes,	Treason,

And other the moſt enormous Crimes.

The Whole being the moſt faithful Narrative ever yet Publiſhed, of the various Executions, and other Puniſhments,

In *ENGLAND, SCOTLAND,* and *IRELAND.*

From the Year 1700, to the preſent Time.

VOL. IV.

How dreadful the Fate of the Wretches who fall,
A Victim to Laws they have broke!
Of Vice, the Beginning is frequently ſmall,
But how fatal at length is the Stroke!
The Contents of theſe Volumes will amply diſplay
The Steps which Offenders have trod:
Learn hence, then, each Reader, the Laws to obey
Of your Country, your King, and your God.

LONDON:
Printed for J. COOKE, at Shakeſpear's Head, No. 10.
Pater-noſter-Row.

The Grassington Murder:

The Story of the infamous Tom Lee

"How dreadful the fate of the wretches who fall,
A victim to laws they have broke!
Of vice, the beginning is frequently small,
But how fatal at length is the stroke!
The contents of these volumes will amply display,
The steps which offenders have trod:
Learn hence, then, each reader, the laws to obey
of your Country, your King and your God."

This rhyme was published in the *Tyburn Chronicle* in 1769 as a stark warning, lest any reader should be tempted to follow in the footsteps of Tom Lee, and contemplate any of the following crimes:

'Bigamy, Murders, Riots, Forgeries, Perjury, Sodomy,
Piracy,
Highway-Robberies, Starving, House-Breaking,
Rapes, Treason, and other most enormous crimes of
Villainy display'd
in all its branches.'

The tale of Tom Lee is something of a legend in the Upper Wharfedale district of Yorkshire. That it is true is indisputable. There is sound documentary evidence describing the events that took place. However, that the most well-known and most believed version of the story is entirely true is perhaps more doubtful. Later renderings of historical events tend by their own nature to evolve, become exaggerated, or are corrupted by the values and fashions of their time. Often, the actual chain of events becomes secondary to the desire to entertain the audience of the time. Coupled with the unavoidable effect of 'Chinese whispers' and the inevitable desire of the storyteller to deliver a rounded, entertaining, and complete tale to his or her audience, it is perhaps not surprising that the one version of the Tom Lee saga to achieve all those things has become the accepted standard – one on which all later retellings are based.

That is not to say that I have dismissed the 'Heather Bell' version out-of-hand. Indeed, it remains the only comprehensive version of events. Nevertheless, its weakness is perhaps also its strength. As I mentioned in the first line of this note, the story now has the status of legend in Grassington and the surrounding communities. A tale so engrained in local culture; it is often mistaken for solid, indisputable fact. There is, at this point, perhaps merit in reminding the reader of the Oxford Dictionary's definition of the word 'Legend':

LEGEND *(noun) /ˈledʒ.ənd'/ Myth. Saga. A traditional story sometimes popularly regarded as historical but not authenticated. Example: "the legend of King Arthur"*

In an attempt to provide the most accurate retelling of the Grassington murder, I have given the most weight to the earliest known versions of events, recorded between 1766 – 1768, since these were not burdened at the time by any commercial need, pressure from publishers, financial ambition, or unquestioning reliance on the oral version which had been passed from generation to generation. I was also delighted to have unearthed the witness statement given on Friday 22nd July 1768 at Lee's trial in York, by John Burnap, Tom Lee's long-suffering servant.

As an added bonus to readers, I have carefully reproduced the entire 'Heather Bell' version of the story, written under that pseudonym by Joseph Robertshaw in 1862, and entitled *Tom Lee: A Wharfedale Tragedy.* Robertshaw, who worked in the textile industry, had been born in Halifax in 1822 or 1823 and no doubt grew up hearing stories of the Grassington murder. He began writing in his mid-thirties, producing several published books, articles, and even a collection of poems. After suffering a stroke in 1886 he retired before passing away in 1894. His keen ear for the Yorkshire accent and dialect is obvious in his published work.

The fact that Robertshaw choose a pseudonym under which to write the story of Tom Lee strongly suggests a fashionable Victorian (and contemporary Yorkshire) influence on his retelling of the tale. His version is no longer available in print, or online. Although dusty, worn copies of his original text may still be found in museums and specialist bookshops. Unfortunately, they tend to be faded, written in the smallest of fonts, and almost unreadable.

Robertshaw's heavily romanticised, picturesque, and moralistic view of Dr Petty's murder was written for the burgeoning tourist market of the mid to late Victorian era (generated largely by the growth of Britain's railway network), and must be read with that context in mind. His book is also, for some part at least, a travelogue. It nevertheless provides a fascinating and entertaining insight into the language, social values, and atmosphere of the time.

The sources used to compile this (hopefully) comprehensive and accurate version of events are listed in chronological order at the end of this book. I am grateful to the work done by the Craven Museum in Skipton, and the various historians and writers listed there. Thank you for your efforts in helping to piece together the story of the Grassington murder and the infamous Thomas Lee.

Mark Bridgeman
www.markbridgemanauthor.co.uk

Introduction

1766 was a volatile year. Just twenty-one years after the Jacobite rebellion in Scotland, the exiled Prince Charles Edward Stuart still yearned for the British throne, hoping to be crowned King Charles III. In the American colonies, British forces continued to quell 'Yankee' uprisings and discontent, while the slave trade saw ever more densely packed ships plying their grim trade across the busy sea lanes of the Atlantic.

Meanwhile, In Upper Wharfedale, life continued very much as it had for many years. Women busied themselves domestically, praying that their husbands would not squander their meagre income from the lead mine on drink or gambling. Life was undoubtedly healthier in the fresh air of the less populated Dales than in the claustrophobic and unsanitary atmosphere of the crowded cities but, for all that, life was none the safer.

Crime was rife in rural England. Even by 1766 the West Riding of Yorkshire was still eighty years away from a unified and recognisable police force. Each town or district employed a local constable, responsible for the collection of fines imposed by the local magistrates, or for undertaking such law enforcement tasks as deemed necessary by that magistrate, or in some instances, by an aggrieved landowner. The constable's salary was paid from a local levy, often in tied accommodation and food, rather than in shillings and pence. These officers received no formal training, had little in the way of protection or equipment – other than perhaps a handy stick or truncheon (known as a 'life preserver') – and often risked danger to life and limb far above and beyond that which would be acceptable today.

Highwaymen (such as the infamous Dick Turpin who had been executed in York just thirty years earlier) lurked in the shadows next to unseen stretches of the public roads, and vagabonds and travelling gypsies robbed unsuspecting travellers along the windy country lanes. Even in the busy market towns such as Grassington, pickpockets plied their trade among the unsuspecting crowds on market day and, as night fell, burglars jemmied open doors and even climbed down chimneys in pursuit of their ill-gotten gains.

With none of our modern crime fighting techniques, forensic science, or even simple advantages like streetlighting, the odds in eighteenth-century England definitely favoured the criminal. In an attempt to counteract this imbalance, punishments were necessarily harsh. Gradually, by way of deterrent, the number of crimes for which a person could be executed increased dramatically. Known as 'The Bloody Code' the number of offences which carried with them the death penalty increased from fifty in

1688 to a mammoth 215 by 1815. These included crimes ranging from murder and arson, at one end of the scale, to wrecking a fishpond, destroying a turnpike road, or wearing a blackened face, at the other end.

Yet, these severe penalties did little to dissuade recidivists from continuing their criminal activities. The small risk of being caught, weighed against the harshness of the sentences, seemed a gamble worth taking. In fact, even when apprehended, there were many squeamish jurors who found the death penalty too distasteful; instead choosing to find the defendant either not guilty, or perhaps opting for a milder punishment. Whilst, by today's standards, these 'lesser' punishments might be considered abhorrent (such as flogging, branding, or transportation to the colonies), at least the criminal might reasonably expect to avoid detection in the first place; or escape the ultimate penalty.

It is against this backdrop that we arrive in the busy and prosperous market town of Grassington in the 1760s.

PART ONE:
The Grassington Murder
The Story of Tom Lee

The notorious tale of Dr Richard Petty's brutal murder at the hands of Thomas Lee from Grassington, begins with Lee's arrival in the town during the early 1750s. Lee, born in the parish of Alston-with-Garrigill in Cumbria in 1731 to Thomas Lee (snr.), a blacksmith, and his wife Sarah, worked in one of the many lead mines on Alston Moor. Typical of the Pennines, the area boasted several lead mines as well as zinc, iron, copper, and coal pits. Importantly, in two notable areas of life, Thomas Lee does not appear to have followed in his father's footsteps. Thomas Lee (snr.) was a blacksmith, while his wife Sarah kept a respectable home. Thomas (jnr.), on the other hand, may have already garnered a reputation for burglary, assault, and highway robbery – not to mention a fearsome temper. The scant records which do exist show a large number of highway robberies in that part of Cumbria around the year 1750. Perhaps Thomas Lee had become too well known In that part of the country and wished to try his luck elsewhere? It may well have been his notoriety which eventually forced him to move to Grassington.

Grassington, already a reasonably wealthy market town, also offered plentiful work for diggers in its burgeoning lead mining industry. The fields outside the town held a rich seam of ore (the remains of early opencast pits can still be seen in the fields surrounding Grassington). Along with employment in the mining industry, came the opportunity to earn a liveable wage. Compared to the lean pickings of farm labourers (two-and-a-half pence per day plus lodgings), there was money to be earned as a 'mine digger'. The opportunity to earn a decent, if hard, living attracted many workers to the district. Conceivably, Lee was simply one of the many miners drawn to Grassington by this opportunity, or perhaps, he wished a change of employer when the lead mines of Alston Moor underwent a change of ownership during this period.

The Rev. Dr Whitaker in his history of Wharfedale, written in 1805, noted with some regret that,

'I do not know of a greater calamity which can befall a village than the discovery of a lead-mine in the neighbourhood.'

He continued his tirade, 'I have only to add, that the miners who carry on these works – a colluvies* from Derbyshire, Alston Moor, etc – have contributed much more to the increase of population than to the improvement of order and good morals.'

*'colluvies' is an archaic word, meaning a collection of foul or filthy matter.

The eccentric Rev. Benjamin Smith from Linton was not much kinder, referring to his flock as little more than 'baptised brutes'.

Grassington Square, 19th Century

Yet, despite this, Thomas Lee seems to have lived in relative prosperity. We know that he was well-established in Grassington by the early 1750s. On 15th November 1754, he married Jane Whitham at St Mary's Church in Ingleton. Jane, the daughter of John Whitham, was illiterate and signed the marriage register with a simple cross. Lee, by contrast, signed his name with a neat and well written signature, and listed his occupation as 'mine digger', revealing that he had received at least some education. He was twenty-three, his bride twenty-two. The couple's first daughter, Mary, was born a year later, with Isabella and Elizabeth following in 1758 and 1761 respectively.

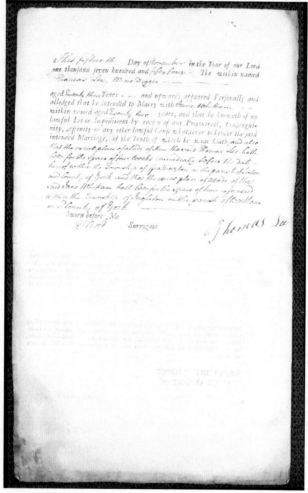

Thomas Lee's signature on his marriage licence

By the early 1760s it appears that Lee was also a regular attendee at cock fights. *The Dalesman* magazine in 1941 noted that 'there was a cock-pit near the village inn at Litton, to which the notorious Tom Lee is supposed to have come often, bringing his cock to fight in the cock fights there.'

Around the same time, he became landlord of the Blue Anchor Inn in Grassington and had also employed a servant named John Burnup. Although 'inns' in the eighteenth-century may have been little more than an unlicenced front parlour, from which homemade and unregulated ales and spirits were sold to the passing public, it does demonstrate that Lee's income was far higher than might be expected simply from his work as a 'mine digger'.

It is also worth noting that although many versions of Tom Lee's story state that he was a blacksmith, with a smiddy in Grassington, and employed John Burnup as an 'apprentice smithy', there is no evidence to confirm this. Perhaps the legend has become conflated over the years, with Lee being confused with his father, who was a blacksmith and shared the same first name. Or, conceivably, Lee (jnr) undertook the occasional minor horseshoeing or buckle repair in a small workshop behind the Blue Anchor Inn. The plaque which now adorns Lee's premises in Main Street, Grassington reads as follows:

'THIS SHOP IS THE ORIGINAL SMIDY
OWNED BY THE NOTORIOUS
TOM LEE
IN THE YEAR 1766

It may well be erroneous. Lee was undoubtedly a 'mine digger', a landlord, a gambler, a highwayman, and a burglar, but there is no evidence to support the assertion that he was a blacksmith.

Whether it was purely a coincidence or not, the number of burglaries on local farmsteads and in roadside robberies (known as Highway robberies) increased markedly in Upper Wharfedale around the years 1750 – 1766. The Yorkshire newspapers reported a 'great number of robberies carried out by a man, but he had no male accomplice, but robbed in company with a woman.' Was this Tom Lee and his wife Jane? It is certainly probable.

Household burglaries also rose, particularly at some of the more traditional farmhouses and cottages possessing larger chimneys and fireplaces, which had been built before the imposition of the *Hearth Tax* in 1663. After that date, smaller chimneys and a reduction in the number of hearths naturally followed. The larger apertures in the older properties offered an easier point of access to the determined housebreaker. Tom Lee was widely suspected of complicity in the increasing spate of break-ins in the district. This was undoubtedly due to his seemingly inexhaustible funds, which enabled him to indulge in his two favourite pastimes – drinking and cock-fighting. Funds which appeared to be far beyond his earnings as a mine digger, or as landlord of a one-room public house.

According to Joseph Robertshaw, writing a century later, 'to this day are to be found strong iron bars in the wide, old-fashioned chimneys of several farmhouses, placed there to prevent Tom's midnight visits.' I wonder if any of these barred chimneys still survive in and around Grassington, and the present occupants appreciate their significance?

Yet, despite there being a good deal of local suspicion, and even acceptance of Lee's guilt, few had the courage to openly confront or accuse him. His reputation for temper, strength, and vindictiveness preceded him. According to an article written in the

Todmorden Advertiser and Hebden Bridge Newsletter, more than a century later, Lee's status had not diminished,

'The history of this murder is still talked about amongst the villagers as if it is of yesterday's occurrence. For there dwelt in Grassington a tall strong man named Tom Lee, who was a character notorious for the depth of his villainy, and for the diabolical nature of his temper; lying, roguery, and thieving were vices in which he was well practiced; he was a constant terror to the neighbourhood; his hand was against every man, and his avaricious spirit would not allow him to pass anything that he could take away without detection, but sometimes he was too daring in his wickedness, and this led to his identity being exposed in more cases than one, though, on account of his revengeful ire, the matters were hushed up, and for many years he escaped the penalty of the law.'

However, circumstances were to soon change for Tom Lee. One day, early in 1766, Lee attempted to rob the bank messenger, who was enroute to Grassington carrying a fortnight's wages for the lead miners there. Lee had armed himself with a bludgeon and placed himself out of sight, next to a lonely section of roadway, where he waited patiently for the unsuspecting traveller to ride by. Fortunately, the bank messenger had armed himself with a pistol. As Lee attacked him, the messenger discharged the pistol into his assailant's upper leg or groin area. According to the 'Heather Bell' version of events the bank's employee, 'lodged a quantity of shot in that part of Tom's person which was covered by the upper parts of his leathern breeches.' The messenger then galloped away towards Grassington, no doubt grateful to have had his life spared, and to report the incident. Lee was left in agony, contemplating his next move. No doubt, a search party would return to look for him. In a state of some confusion and no doubt in a great deal of pain, he took some time to gather his thoughts before eventually staggering away to the moor, where he hid amongst the rocks until nightfall.

The *Todmorden Advertiser and Hebden Bridge Newsletter* continues the story,

'Being in great pain he at last ventured to go to Grassington. The inhabitants had, by this time, all heard of the dastardly affair, and, for anything he knew, all suspected him of being the culprit; nevertheless, he felt he must run all risks, and go to the doctor for relief, or else die. The doctor's name was Petty.'

Dr Richard Petty had been born at Colne, Lancashire, in 1735. His father, John Petty had moved from the village of Dent, in the Lake District. The family were almost certainly related to the well-known Pettys of Craven.

Dr Petty's Saw Case (courtesy of the Craven Museum)

John Petty had married Mary Walton at Colne during 1732 and by way of marriage he became the landlord of the Hole-in-the-Wall Inn on the High Street in Colne. Mary had inherited the Inn from her father George Walton. However, in 1732, a wife was considered a *feme covert* under English Common Law, meaning she was not able to own property in her own right. The Inn automatically fell under the ownership of her new husband. This imbalance in the law was not corrected until the introduction of the *Married Woman's Property Act 1882.*

It seems that John Petty had a keen interest in cock fighting. This barbaric sport was a popular form of entertainment at that time, and as such, 'cockpits' were often attached to inns. Such was the case at the

Hole-in-the-Wall Inn. During June 1764 a bill-poster was displayed, announcing a cockfight 'Yorkshire versus Lancashire' at Petty's Pit, Colne'. Richard Petty was familiar with cock fighting, no doubt inheriting his interest from his father. Unfortunately, he was also attracted to the gambling that was associated with it. This twin obsession was to indirectly lead to Dr Petty's violent death in 1766.

The young Richard Petty studied hard and became an apothecary, eventually arriving in Grassington to begin practising as a doctor around 1765. It is most likely that he took over the rounds of Dr John Hawkridge (who described himself as 'Surgeon, Man Midwife and Apothecary'). Dr Hawkridge retired from Grassington in 1765 and moved to Otley.

Returning to the events of the morning following Lee's botched robbery of the lead mine wages, the story is taken up once more by the newspaper,

'The doctor's name was Petty; he was noted for his talents and his benevolence, and was held in great respect throughout the whole of Upper Wharfedale – from Bolton to Buckden his name was familiar. Tom Lee had often been to him before, but never with so desperate a case as this last one; however, under skilful treatment Lee was soon all right again, but this was at the cost of a secret that troubled him day and night. His guilt was well known to the doctor, and at that time he was liable to suffer public capital punishment at York Prison for the offence he had committed, therefore his life was in the hands of his physician in more senses than life usually is.'

By the time this story appeared in the *Todmorden Advertiser* in 1876, public executions had been banned. The final public hanging in Britain had taken place in London eight years earlier, in 1868, when Michael Barrett had been executed for the 'Fenian Bombing Outrage' at Clerkenwell. York's last public hanging took place a great deal earlier, in 1801. This disparity was not due to a more enlightened attitude among Yorkshire's population, but purely as a commercial measure. It had been decided that public executions (which were carried out at Knavesmire, on the city's boundary) were discouraging visitors and tradesmen from entering the city.

Meanwhile, the *Todmorden Advertiser* continued its narrative,

'Lee knew the doctor could bring him to the gallows if he were so inclined, and, as he brooded over this, the evil spirit which dwelt within him waxed strong in its influence, and the demon whispered, "Kill the doctor." He resolved to do so. This resolution was strengthened by the doctor often making Lee the butt of his jokes, and throwing out hints in reference to the affair.'

It is at this point in the retelling of the story that the 'Heather Bell' version recorded by Joseph Robertshaw differs from other, earlier descriptions. The complete 'Heather Bell' version is reproduced later in the book.

On Easter Tuesday, 1st April 1766, Tom Lee and Dr Petty both attended the cock fighting in the village of Kettlewell. The event, known as the 'Kettlewell Cockings' presented both men with the opportunity to drink and gamble to their hearts' content. It is conceivable that Lee attended with Dr Petty, not as friends, but because he wished to ensure that the doctor did not suddenly become loose-tongued under the influence of alcohol, and mention Lee's involvement in the attempted robbery of the lead mine wages. Lee, it seems, had managed to persuade Dr Petty to remain silent so far, but was clearly worried that his guilty secret would eventually be divulged by the doctor.

Perhaps Lee had a much darker plan in mind, and had already premeditated a permanent solution to his problem.

According to witnesses, Dr Petty was successful at the cock fight and won a sizeable sum of money. Both men were seen to leave together on horseback. Presumably celebrating, the pair first called in at Israel Simpson's Inn in Kettlewell, followed by the Anglers' Inn at Kilnsey, owned by Henry Ovington.

Contemporary Illustration of a Fighting Game Cock

The popular Inn had been established in 1760 and the building still exists today, although it is now a holiday home. Above the front door is a date stone marked 'H O E 1768'.

The two men were served in the Anglers' Inn by Henry Ovington himself. His assistant, John Inman, was also present. Tom Lee and Dr Petty were served with two 'jacks' of rum and two pints of punch. A 'jack', in northern England equates to a quarter-pint, with a 'jill' being a half-pint. This now redundant drinks measure is also the original source of the word 'jackpot'.

Formerly the Anglers Inn at Kilnsey

The Keystone above the old Anglers Inn in Kilnsey

Dr Petty also asked the landlord for some paper in which he wished to wrap his winnings from the Kettlewell Cockings. He was given an old newspaper advertisement for a cock fight. Dr Petty then carefully folded his prize money inside the sheet of newspaper, apparently in clear view of everyone present, since Henry Ovington noticed that, even in the candlelight, that at least some of the coins were gold. At that time, the glint of a gold coin in someone's possession would have caught an onlooker's eye in the way perhaps a wad of £50 notes might today. Henry Ovington thought Dr Petty's bounty amounted to either four guineas and two half-guineas (approximately £1,200 today), or four shillings and six pence (£56 today). The larger amount seems the more likely one to take such trouble in concealing, and would have been a handsome reward for any highwayman. Dr Petty was clearly wise to take precautions.

After leaving the Angler's Inn together, the two men headed south along Grass Wood Lane towards Grassington. They stopped again at Henry Ellis's Inn in the small village of Conistone, where they apparently drank a pint of rum. As Lee and Dr Petty left, 'both men appeared to be full of liquor' (according to evidence given later at the inquest by Henry Ellis). Lee himself confessed that he and the doctor were 'pretty well drunk', but that he was, 'the full soberer of the two'.

According to Lee's version of events (later deponed on oath), the two men began racing each other along the track until they reached the hill in Grass Wood. Lee claimed that he then called out to the doctor, 'pull up your horse, before one of us is thrown from the saddle and breaks our neck.' Lee slowed to a canter, he maintained, but Dr Petty refused to break gallop and continued onwards towards Grassington until he was out of site. Based on this testimony from Lee, he was the last person to see Dr Petty alive.

Shortly after this, the doctor's riderless horse cantered back to his home in Grassington. A few minutes later, Tom Lee returned to the Blue Anchor Inn, to be met by his wife, Jane, and servant, John Burnup. Lee informed Burnup that he had beaten the doctor back to town, but that the doctor would no doubt be home shortly, bringing with him the news of his winnings at the cock fight.

The road through Grass Wood

At approximately 4am in the early hours of the following morning (Wednesday 2nd April 1766), Christopher Mitton, the blacksmith from the village of Starbotton, knocked at the Blue Anchor Inn to enquire if Dr Petty was still with Lee. Mitton needed the doctor to return urgently to Starbotton with him to tend to his sick wife. Mitton explained that he had called at the doctor's house, but had received no answer. John Burnup was forced to rouse Lee from his slumber, with Christopher Mitton's request. However, Lee informed him that he had left the doctor on the outskirts of town late the previous evening, and had no idea where he was.

With the arrival of daylight, the mystery only deepened. There was still no sign of the doctor nor any clue as to his absence. Rumour and speculation began to spread quickly. Had Dr Petty slipped from his horse? Had he fallen into the river and drowned? The road which the doctor and Tom Lee had taken the previous night passed through Grass Wood. However, the track was bordered by thick bushes and trees, making it unlikely that a man could easily fall from a horse into the nearby River Wharfe. Besides, the track only closely bordered the river in a handful of places. When asked, Tom Lee speculated that it was unlikely that the doctor could have been thrown into the river, as the track was too thickly wooded. He added that, if somehow Dr Petty had accidently fallen into the water, ropes would be needed to mount any search.

Nevertheless, many others in Grassington thought the doctor had simply over celebrated his good fortune at the cock fights, and would eventually emerge from the Lee's parlour at the Blue Anchor Inn, bleary eyed, sheepish, and hungover.

Twenty-four hours passed, yet there was still no sign of the town's doctor. On Thursday morning it was decided by the townsfolk of Grassington that Tom Lee would be the ideal person to search for the much-loved Dr Petty, since Lee had been the last person to have seen the doctor and knew the route he had supposedly taken. Tom Lee was no doubt more than pleased to be asked, as this request seemed to indicate he was not suspected of any foul play in the doctor's unexplained disappearance. Lee was sent as far as the cockpit in Kettlewell, then asked to retrace his and the doctor's steps back to Grassington. When he reached Conistone, Lee called in again at Henry Ellis's Inn, and (according to Mary Ellis, the landlord's wife) he appeared to be in good spirits. Lee was asked if his apparent good mood was because he had succeeded in finding the doctor, to which he answered, 'No, but I wish I had.'

Word of his son's disappearance had been sent to John Petty in Colne and he arrived in Grassington on Friday 4th April to help with the search. John Petty generously paid the expenses incurred in the quest for his son, and keep a detailed statement which he headed 'An Account of money laid out for my deceased son at Grassington'. The statement details various payments for travel expenses to and from Grassington, and for evidence given by various parties. These records are now held at the Craven Museum in Skipton.

Grassington Square

Meanwhile, Lee returned empty handed from his search for Dr Petty. However, his untroubled demeanour must have aroused some suspicions in the town as he was asked, on Tuesday 15th April, to give a statement to the local magistrates Rev. Thomas Collins and Edward Leedes at the Skipton Sessions.

After explaining the circumstances of their visits to the various hostelries on the return journey from Kettlewell to Grassington, Lee repeated his version of events, testifying that he and Dr Petty had parted company on the road through Grass Wood and that the doctor had ridden on ahead towards home. In the stillness of the night, Lee stated, he was certain he could hear the doctor's Galloway horse a good way in front of him all the way back to Grassington (The Galloway was a large and sturdy breed of pony, distinctive and reliable. Sadly, the strain is now extinct through crossbreeding).

Although Lee claimed he was certain that he could hear the sound of Dr Petty's Galloway a few hundred yards ahead of him on the track, he also conceded that he did not actually see Dr Petty when he himself arrived back in Grassington. Lee, instead, admitted to the magistrate that he was probably the last person 'to be in Dr Petty's company, before he met his unknown fate.'

Lee's explanation does not appear to have satisfied the authorities. According to a later account by the prolific Yorkshire writer Edmund Bogg (1851 – 1931), writing in his 1904 guide to the area, *Higher Wharfedale*, the net was closing in on Thomas Lee,

'Rather more than a century has fled since "Tom Lee" chose this spot for the final hiding-place of his victim. On two occasions had the doctor's body been secreted; but the murderer was still fearful lest its hiding-place should be discovered.

Edmund Bogg

Just after midnight, when all at Grassington but the guilty pair had retired to rest, Lee, accompanied by his wife and leading a pony, glided out of the village. Dark storm-clouds swept across the moor, obscuring the light of the moon. Arriving at the solitary grave, he again unearthed his victim, which he placed in a sack and threw across the pony's back, crossed the moors above Hebden, and on to Burnsall, where the body, attached to large stones, was hurled into the river.

Retribution was afoot and on the murderer's track. That night a young man from Grassington, who, visiting his lady-love, had lingered as lovers will, was returning home by the banks of the river, lost in a reverie of bliss, when he was arrested by the sound of a voice exclaiming, "That thief, tha'll show his legs; cover em up!" Peering down from the opposite bank, he heard the splash of the falling body; just at that moment the clouds parted and the moon shone full on the guilty pair. The chain of evidence was fast closing round the murderer, for, as the young man proceeded to Grassington, he soliloquized: "Begow, but this licks me, it dew, I cud almost sweer that it wur Tom Lee an' 'is wife".'

Three days later, Lee was arrested on suspicion of murdering Dr Petty and committed to York Prison to await the inquest and, hopefully, the discovery of the doctor's body.

Although, during the eighteenth century, a murder trial could be held without the victim's body, formal inquest proceedings could not. Inquests were normally held as soon after the discovery of the body as possible. Usually within twenty-four to forty-eight hours. The reason was very much a practical one. Inquest jurors were expected to view the corpse - *super visum corporis* (on view of the body) as a precursor to the proceedings. In an era before electricity, and the ability to effectively store a body at cold temperature, the decaying condition of the corpse must have been unpleasant in the extreme – especially during the summer months. Due to the lack of large public buildings, inquests were often help in the parlours of public houses, as these provided accommodation for any visiting officials, and usually a large kitchen table on which to display the body. The inquest into the death of Dr Petty would be no exception; the proceedings were held in a small airless room at the Bridge Tavern, which must have been an uncomfortable experience for everyone involved.

However, before the formal inquest could begin, the body of Dr Petty would need to surface. This it did, quite literally, on Thursday 1st May 1766, one month after the doctor's strange disappearance.

On that Thursday morning, a local lady, Ann Grieve, was walking on the bank of the River Wharfe at Burnsall, three miles downstream from Grassington. She happened to notice something floating in the water. It appeared to be cloth or sacking of some description, wrapped around a larger object. After fetching her husband William and another man named William Airton, they waded into the water and pulled the object to shore. It was the body of Dr Richard Petty, which they instantly recognised. Although the doctor had been missing for a month, his corpse appeared to be reasonably well preserved.

An immediate inquest was ordered, so that a formal identification could be made, and the injuries on the body viewed by the coroner and jurors. The coroner, John Lobley, was summoned from his home twenty miles away, in the small town of Balidon on the outskirts of Bradford, along with Dr John Wainman from Skipton. Fifteen jurors were hastily gathered from the surrounding villages of Grassington, Linton, Hebden, and Burnsall-with-Thorpe. Among the jurors were David Swaile, a solicitor from Grassington, and Richard Fountaine, Jr, from Linton. Despite the seemingly hasty arrangements, those eligible to serve as jurors were carefully selected according to the guidelines laid out in *The Act for the Better Regulation of Juries 1730*. All jurors were required to be 'Honest and lawful men aged 21 -70, freeholders, or men who held land by lease to the minimum value of £20 per annum, indifferent to the subject matter of the inquiry, and able to write their names legibly at the Inquisition.' The act also levied a fine of between £2 - £5 for non-attendance (equivalent to approximately £450 - £1,000 today, which, coincidentally, is comparable to the applicable fine for a juror's non-attendance now), although it also sought to 'not limit the patience of same man, by his being called more than once every two years.'

Alongside the doctor and the members of the jury, John Lobley the coroner was also expected to examine the body to decide if 'decease had occurred accidently by horse', from 'accident by drowning', or by 'a sudden visitation from God'. If none of these appeared to be the cause of death, then the coroner was dutybound to seek a more sinister conclusion in his examination of the corpse, including, 'Any signs of strangling around the neck, or of cords tied about the limbs.' In addition, the jurors were expected to 'view all wounds on the body'. A request was made to Thomas Lee's associate, John Bownass, to give evidence at the inquest; however, Bownass later stated to colleagues that, 'I knew nothing of the matter, so the jury immediately dismissed me.'

Once this hastily arranged inquest had opened and the body viewed, it was quickly adjourned to allow Rev. Matthew Knowles to oversee the burial of Dr Petty at St Wilfrid's Church in Burnsall. Rev. Knowles had taken the living at St Wilfrid's twelve years earlier, and the funeral of Dr Petty was surely the most dramatic and sensational interment to take place during his tenure in the Parish. A small headstone was then placed over the doctor's grave, which read simply 'R.P. 1766'.

Although the church of St Wilfrid's is little changed today (and is an interesting and enlightening place to visit), the doctor's gravestone seems to have been destroyed or lost at some point. The church records do not indicate where the doctor was buried, nor what became of his headstone. The only remaining clue to the event is an entry in the Parish burial register (which is available to view on the bookcase inside the church), and which reads simply:

'Petty, Richard 3rd May 1766 Found in the water (buried) 3a/394'

The time served in the 'living' at St Wilfrid's by the Rev. Matthew Knowles is engraved on a wooden board, on the wall behind the font:

'1754 MATTHEW KNOWLES M.A.'

Rev. Knowles remained at St Wilfrid's until his death in 1776.

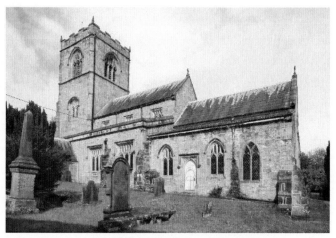

St Wilfrid's Church, Burnsall

Following the funeral of Dr Petty, the adjourned inquest was reconvened in Grassington on Monday 19th May 1766. Without a surgeon since the disappearance of Dr Petty, Dr Wainman had been persuaded to return to Grassington – seemingly against his will - not only to testify at the inquest, but to temporarily take up medical duties in the town. His obituary in the September 1794 edition of *Gentleman's Magazine* reads as follows,

'It was rather to comply with the wishes of others, than his own inclination, that he submitted to sit down as surgeon and apothecary in the humble situation of his native place. In a neighbourhood so thinly peopled, where trade has not yet spread affluence, nor the arts of civilisation polished the general manners or enlarged the sentiments of the inhabitants.'

The positive identification of Dr Petty's body was the first point of order at the reconvened inquest. This transpired to be a relatively easy task. The material in which the doctor's body had been wrapped had clearly been buried in the ground prior to being thrown into the River Wharfe. There were many muddy, soil marks on the cloth, which were thought to be peat; and which helped to explain the lack of decomposition to the body. Peat, due to its waterlogged state, contains very little oxygen. This anaerobic state markedly slows down the rate at which organic material decomposes.

Ann Grieve, who had first spotted the body in the River Wharfe, was able to identify the corpse as that of Dr Petty, as were several others present. In addition, an examination of the victim's waistcoat pocket revealed several receipts and bills. These were shown to the Grassington lawyer Thomas Brown, who confirmed that the items clearly belonged to Dr Petty. Importantly, however, the cockfighting bill-poster advertisement (in which Dr Petty had alleged wrapped his winnings) was not present on the body. Did this indicate that robbery rather than revenge was the motive behind the doctor's tragic death?

The medical evidence came from Dr Wainman, who testified that he could find no bruises or wounds on the body which – in his opinion – would account for Dr Petty's demise. Having been unable to state a definite cause of death, Dr Wainman examined the victim's clothing. He concluded that the body had only been in the water for a short period of time, and had clearly been moved there from some other place. He also added the following remark to the inquest,

'What could induce anyone to bring a stinking body into the water, unless that person or persons were an accessory in his death? Hence I judge some violence has been offered him, but by whom I cannot say.'

Thomas Lee was not asked to give evidence at the inquest (he was still languishing in a cell at York Castle at the time, and had been since his arrest). Neither were Lee's servant John Burnup, nor his known associates John Bownass, or John Hulley, called to provide testimony.

Coroner John Lobley then requested that the inquest jury retire and consider their verdict. Should Thomas Lee be sent to the next Assizes in York to face trial for the murder of Dr Petty, or not? After a short deliberation the jurors returned and informed the coroner that he should indeed face trial. According to the surviving records of the inquest, the jury found as follows,

'That Richard Petty on Tuesday 1st April went from Grassington to Kettlewell to a cock fight and was supposed to have won money, and on his return to Grassington was in company with Tom Lee or some other person or persons unknown, and that the said Richard Petty was murdered by the said Thomas Lee or some other person or persons unknown.'

An order was then given by the coroner for Tom Lee to face trial at the Yorkshire Summer Assizes in July for the murder of Dr Petty. Preparations were made for the trial, which included ensuring that Henry Ovington, William Airton, Thomas Brown, Mary Ellis, and Dr Wainman were bound over to give evidence, at a penalty of £20 (£4,500 today) should they fail to appear. John Inman, the Constable of Burnsall, 'entered into his own recognizances', to the sum of £40, should he fail to successfully arrange the prosecution.

The Trial Of Thomas Lee

The date of the Yorkshire Summer Assizes was set for Friday 18th July, to be held in York, and expected to last for two days. Assizes were held on a quarterly basis in various locations around the country and exercised both civil and criminal jurisdiction, although the majority of the cases dealt with were of a criminal nature. Originally established in 1166 by King Henry II, as a trial by grand assize of twelve knights to oversee land disputes, the system was an ancient one, deriving its name from the old French word 'assise', meaning 'meeting'. As Thomas Lee prepared to face his trial in York in July 1766, the system of assize sessions was marking its 600th anniversary. However, it is doubtful that Lee, would have been in the mood to celebrate.

Surprisingly, the assize court system was not abolished until the passing of the *Courts Act 1971*, which saw quarterly sessions replaced with a single permanent Crown Court.

Meanwhile in Upper Wharfedale, last-minute attempts were being made to consolidate the admittedly circumstantial evidence against Thomas Lee. Just eight days before his impending trial, magistrates were at last able to obtain a statement from Lee's servant, John Burnup. Burnup was bound over in the sum of £40 to give evidence at the trial. Described in his summons to appear as a 'miner', and not as Lee's servant, it is possible that John Burnup had been acquainted with Lee in Alston-with-Garrigill in Cumbria, before the latter's move to Grassington. Burnup was a common surname in Cumbria at that time.

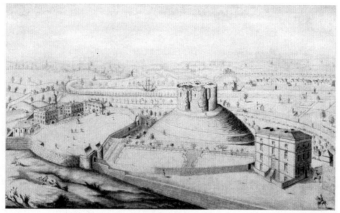

York Prison

The day of the assizes arrived, with three cases due to be tried. That of a man named Robert Pawson for sheep stealing, John Skipwith for murder, and Thomas Lee for the murder of Dr Petty. Lee's charge was read to the Grand Jury as follows:

'That Thomas Lee, not having the fear of God before his eyes, but being moved and seduced by the instigation of the Devil, lade an assault on Richard

Petty, and that Lee with both his hands most violently did squeeze and bruise the throat and neck of Dr Petty, and did feloniously, wilfully and of malice aforethought, strangle, suffocate, kill and murder Dr Petty, of which by strangling and suffocation Dr Petty then and there instantly died, against the peace of our Lord the King, his Crown and dignity.'

The charge appears to be at odds with the evidence given by Dr Wainman at the adjourned inquest two months earlier, who (as mentioned previously) testified that he had found no bruises or wounds on the body which he thought could have been responsible for Dr Petty's demise. Since Dr Petty had been interred immediately following the first inquest, meaning there had been no opportunity for any further examination of the body, this discrepancy indicates one of three possibilities.

1. Either Dr Wainman had been mistaken or his examination had not been thorough enough (remember, he had been deeply unenthusiastic at being asked to take up the position of doctor in Grassington).

2. A further postmortem was actually carried out, but no records remain, or,

3. That the Crown exaggerated the evidence against Thomas Lee in an effort to obtain a conviction. Perversely, this tactic often worked against the

prosecution, as jurors frequently acquitted the accused person out of sheer stubbornness, combined with their fatigue and general distaste of the death penalty.

The technicalities of the process are worth mentioning at this juncture. In order for the Crown to obtain a conviction against Lee, the Grand Jury would need to be convinced that there was indeed a *prima facie* case to answer. This would then lead to Lee being tried before a petty jury for conviction and sentencing. This two-part process offered two safeguards. One for the Crown, one for the accused. If the Grand Jury found that there was no case to answer, Lee would be acquitted; but could be re-tried should further evidence come to light. If, however, he was sent to face a petty trial and subsequently acquitted, legal precedent would mean he could not face another trial, even if further evidence came to light. Even by 1766, the principal of *'autrefois acquit'* (known better in the modern era as 'double jeopardy'), had already been a pillar of English law for almost 500 years. It would remain so for a further two-and-a-half centuries until the passing of the *Criminal Justice Act 2003*.

Returning to Lee's hearing on the 19th and 20th July 1766, testimony was given by Christopher Mitton (the Starbotton blacksmith), who confirmed that he had called at the Blue Anchor Inn at 4am, on the morning of Dr Petty's disappearance, and had been told by Lee that the doctor was not there. Next came the evidence of Margaret Calvert from Addingham, who had been in Kettlewell on the night of the cockfight. She confirmed that Lee and Dr Petty had called at the house of Israel Simpson for a drink, following the cockfight.

The crucial evidence of Lee's servant John Burnup came next. Burnup confirmed to the Grand Jury that Lee had returned to the Blue Anchor on the evening of Easter Tuesday, at about 9pm. He also confirmed that Christopher Mitton had called, looking for the doctor, at 4am in the early hours of the following morning. Burnup then explained that he and the accused man had later been involved in the search for Dr Petty, with both men finding a glove in the river. According to the evidence of the next witness, Mr James Swaile's maid, the gloves belonged to her master, who had lent them to Dr Petty on one of the doctor's previous visits.

In a potentially damaging piece of evidence, John Burnup testified that he had overheard Lee saying to James Swaile's maid that, 'If Dr Petty had been murdered, then he (Lee) had himself murdered the doctor, unless the Devil had gone with him.' This apparently damaging confession was typical of Lee's temper and, according to Burnup's evidence, Lee's wife immediately pulled him to one side and supposedly warned him about the tone of his remarks.

Nevertheless, despite these seemingly damaging remarks made by Lee, the Grand Jury decided to acquit him. The *Leeds Intelligencer*, writing on the Tuesday following the completion of the trial, reported that,

'On Saturday last the Assize ended at York, which proved a maiden one. The indictment against Thomas Lee on suspicion of murdering Mr Richard Petty of Grassington in Craven, was not found. Robert Pawson, for sheep stealing, was ordered to be transported for seven years; and John Skipwith, on suspicion of the murder of John Eckles, was acquitted.'

Another periodical, the *Leeds Courant*, reported that Lee was, 'honourably acquitted by the Grand Jury', however, it could hardly be described as that. The members of the jury merely thought there was insufficient evidence for the case against Lee to be taken to the next stage. As mentioned earlier, rather than risking a further trial, the door was left ajar for a future prosecution should further evidence arise.

Following the trial, Tom Lee was released and he returned to the Blue Anchor Inn in Grassington. It seems that his servant John Burnup left Lee's employment shortly afterwards and went into service in the County of Durham. No doubt the atmosphere at the Blue Anchor was not a pleasant one for Burnup, following his frank testimony in court. Knowing Lee's temper and demeanour better than almost anyone else, it was probably a wise choice.

The legend that has evolved alongside the story tells us that as Lee was returning to Grassington on 21st July, the glorious summer weather abruptly changed, and the Heavens suddenly opened to direct God's displeasure at his escape from justice. Indeed, it was recorded in the *Leeds Intelligencer* on 29th July that,

'Yesterday sennight (an archaic noun meaning a week ago) there fell at Skipton-in-Craven a violent storm of rain, attended with terrible shocks of thunder and lightning, that has ever been on the memory of the oldest man there. The lightning fell upon the pinnacle at the east-end of the Church steeple, beat down the weathercock; and tore asunder several of the large stones at the bottom of the pinnacle; it also broke three or four windows, and damaged the stone mullions in which they were fixed.'

In fact, the truth is slightly more prosaic. The weather had been atrocious throughout the whole of the north of England for the previous two weeks, resulting in widespread damage and destruction.

According to the *Leeds Intelligencer*,

'On the 13th July, a Woman was struck dead by lightning, at Sawley near Ripon, and two of her companions, who were in the House with her, were much scorched. A horse was also struck dead, at Coal-hill, near Bramley, in this Parish; and several trees were split in different parts of the country. On Saturday last, a cart-driver was riding his cart through violent storms, near Batley, when the horses took fright, which endeavoured him to stop, he was thrown down, and the wheels going over his body, killed him on the spot.'

'Newcastle, July 26. On Monday we had several loud claps of thunder, with very heavy showers of rain; the water overflowed the channels. At Stannington, the chimneys were thrown down, the windows broke, the china overturned, and two dogs killed.'

Even as far north as Berwick it was reported that during July,

'They had the heaviest during last week, with thunder and lightning, ever known at that place; the lightning struck the gallows and shivered it all to pieces, a man was close by, loading his cart, but received no hurt.'

As is often the case with an event that evolves into legend and is handed down orally, dates blur, and more than one story frequently merges into another.

1766 – 1768

Following his acquittal, Tom Lee returned to Grassington no doubt a relieved man. Men had been convicted of murder before on far less circumstantial evidence than that presented to the Grand Jury in York. Several witnesses had seen Lee with Dr Petty on the night of his murder. The doctor was known to have won a great deal of money, which was not in his pockets when his body was eventually discovered, and Lee had a fearsome reputation locally as a man with a violent temper who may have been involved in robberies (remember many local householders had placed iron bars in their chimney flues to prevent burglary).

Outwardly at least, the next two years passed quietly for Tom Lee. His son (Thomas Junior) was baptised at St Michael's Church in Linton. Conceivably Lee believed that the truth of what really happened on the night of Dr Petty's disappearance would remain known only to those involved. Perhaps, the only doubt lingering in Lee's mind was that of confidence. Could he trust those who knew, to keep their guilty secret? Or, perhaps one of the witnesses present at the Inn might remember a crucial detail not previously revealed?

St. Michael's, Linton

One question worth considering, is whether Tom Lee continued with his criminal activities. Would he have been foolish enough to continue with his gambling, highway robberies, or house burglaries? The simple answer is, we do not know.

Cockfighting did continue at Kettlewell, and elsewhere. Whether Lee attended, gambling his ill-gotten gains, is not known. Although cockfighting was widely disapproved off, and generally frowned upon by the church and polite society, it would not actually be made illegal until 1835. During the eighteenth century it was supposedly governed by 'breach of the peace' regulations; however, these were widely ignored, and its resulting effect on society can be gathered from this *Newcastle Courant* article dated 1784,

Hogarth - Cockfighting

'This court takes into most serious consideration the pernicious consequences of cock fighting within this country, in open violation of the known laws of this kingdom, and tending directly to corrupt the morals of the people, already too much depraved, and to habituate them to a course of idleness and debauchery, by which the community is not only deprived of the work of many hundred able and useful hands (and frequently at those seasons of the year when it is most wanted) but also becomes burthened with the maintenance of the wives and children of such idle persons thus reduced to poverty and distress.'

It is doubtful that Tom Lee, or anyone else, took heed of these pleas.

Meanwhile, house burglaries and highway robberies persisted in Wharfedale. Again, there is no direct evidence to prove Lee's involvement. However, perhaps the most interesting events to occur (events which have not been mentioned in any previous account of the Grassington murder), are the untimely deaths of both Henry Ellis and his son. As mentioned earlier, Henry Ellis was the landlord of a small inn in Conistone. Tom Lee and Dr Petty had called there for a drink on the night of the doctor's disappearance. Henry Ellis had been the last witness to see Dr Petty alive (other than the person who killed him), and almost certainly the final person to observe Lee and the doctor together.

St. Mary's Church, Conistone

According to the parish burial records of St Mary's Church in Conistone, Henry Ellis died just two months after Lee's release from York Prison. He was buried at St Mary's on 21st September. A year later, on 5th November 1767, his son (Henry junior) also died suddenly and was buried next to his father. Was this merely an unfortunate coincidence, or Tom Lee coldheartedly removing witnesses to his crime? There are no records to indicate how either man died. If Tom Lee did ruthlessly dispose of these two men, it would elevate his status from the Grassington murderer to that of the Grassington serial killer.

With Henry Ellis and his son now dead, perhaps Lee felt a little more secure. However, Ellis's widow, Mary, still survived and would be able to testify in any future trial. Perhaps Lee was distracted instead by the looming spectre of his ex-servant John Burnup, who had since moved away. Burnup was now beyond Lee's control and influence.

The first warning of Burnup's troubled conscience came shortly after Lee's acquittal. Enroute to the County of Durham, Burnup travelled via Wharfedale. In order to break the journey, he stayed a night with Christopher Mitton, the blacksmith at Starbotton. It appears that the two men discussed the case and Burnup, his tongue undoubtedly loosened by alcohol, told Mitton that Dr Petty's hat had been removed from his body, by the four people present during the murder. According to Burnup, the hat was then cut into four pieces. Each of the four participants in the crime then threw a piece of the doctor's hat into the fire and watched them disintegrate into unrecognisable ashes - perhaps in some murderous ritual or solemn bond of secrecy. Burnup claimed that the four people present were himself, Thomas Lee, Lee's wife Jane, and John Bownass.

Possibly Christopher Mitton did not take Burnup's 'confession' seriously, or a sober Burnup merely denied his drunken outpourings the following day. Nothing more was to happen for two years, until the second anniversary of Dr Petty's death once again wrestled with John Burnup's conscience.

During March of 1768, it appears that John Burnup's conscience finally got the better of him. He approached his master in Durham, cautiously implying that he knew more about the killing of Dr Petty two years earlier, than he had previously disclosed. He was advised to make a formal statement before a magistrate. Burnup was then taken before Peter Overend, a West Riding magistrate, who resided in Bentham, close to Kirkby Lonsdale. Burnup's testimony would prove devastating for Tom Lee.

After swearing on the bible that his statement would be a true one, Burnup revealed that he had been at the Blue Anchor Inn in Grassington on the night that Lee had returned alone from the Kettlewell cockfight in 1766. He stated to Peter Overend that, when Lee arrived at the Blue Anchor, he informed his wife, Jane, that he and John Bownass had killed Dr Petty at the far end of Grass Wood. Jane replied, 'Keep your counsel and this will never be known.' Burnup repeated the story he had told Christopher Mitton in 1766, that the doctor's hat had been cut into pieces and burnt. Next, Burnup addressed the discovery of Dr Petty's gloves on the riverbank by the Linton stepping stones. According to his testimony, Jane Lee and her mother Isabel Whitman carefully placed the gloves close to the stepping stones just before the search was made for the doctor. Tom Lee then ordered Burnup to join the search and conveniently 'find' one of the gloves. Lee himself would then miraculously chance upon the other glove by a willow tree on the bank, thus freeing the Lees from the suspicion of any involvement in the doctor's murder.

Linton Stones

Burnup also claimed that he had overheard Lee discussing with his wife how to silence the other individuals involved in the death of Dr Petty. However, he was unable to get close enough to determine Lee's exact plans, for fear of being discovered by Lee and murdered himself.

He added that, after Lee had first been arrested, his wife travelled to York to visit him in prison. On her return she warned Burnup that if he told anyone about what he had overheard, her husband would return home and kill him. Jane Lee also added that, due to Lee's fear of its discovery, Dr Petty's body had been taken from the spot in the long reeds where it had been originally left and conveyed deeper into Grass Wood, where it was buried between two large grey stones. However, still fearing its discovery, and with Tom Lee now remanded in York Prison, Jane Lee and John Bownass then coerced Burnup into assisting them in moving the body once more. This time, in the dead of the night, the doctor's corpse was moved into an area known locally as the Mire, in Grassington Old Pasture, where it was reburied. According to Burnup's statement, he was offered a half-guinea (approximately £100 today) for his troubles, and threatened with his own murder if he refused to help, or ever spoke of what had happened that night.

In light of Burnup's testimony, the magistrate also called Christopher Mitton to Bentham to make a statement. Mitton recalled the conversation between himself and Burnup immediately after the York Summer Assizes of 1766, in which Burnup had told him about the doctor's gloves and about his impression that four people were involved in Dr Petty's murder; one of whom Mitton assumed to be Jane Lee.

This was enough for the magistrate, and on Sunday 27th March 1768 (almost two years after the murder of Dr Petty), he ordered the arrest of Tom Lee for a second time.

The *Leeds Intelligencer* recorded the arrest in their issue of 12th April,

'He was committed for the same crime in April 1766, but for want of evidence at the Summer Assize following, no bill was found against him. But is now said a young man has made some discovery, which is the cause of his being again committed. The further arrests of John Burnup, John Hulley, and John Bownass were also made on April 5th on suspicion of being concerned in removing the body of Richard Petty, apothecary, of Grassington in Craven, and the men were charged on oath.'

Some details of the expenses involved in bringing Lee, his fellow conspirators, and various witnesses, to York were donated to the Craven Museum in Skipton in 1929, by Mr J.C. Scott from Ilkley. Although not on public display, the accounts are held in the museum's archives. The records were meticulously collated by Richard Petty's father, John, and were then endorsed by the signature of Peter Overend, the magistrate, and 'Thomas Brown and David Swaile, Constables of Grassington'. They are a fascinating insight into the procedures of the period, and also a testament to the thoroughness of John Petty's search for justice in the murder of his son.

A travelling allowance of a shilling per mile was paid for each rider and each horse:

'1768, 27th March
Expenses
Attending the taking and conducting of Thom. Lee to the Castle of York on suspicion of murdering Rich'd Pety, Apothecary, late of Grassington'

The accounts list the names of many witnesses, including Henry Ovington, Christopher Lawson, James Howarth, William Robinson, John Dolphin, Anthony Hawley, and Thomas Davis.

1768, 5th April
Allowance for conducting to the Castle of York:

Thomas Lee to York Castle from Skipton
Being 43 Miles

John Hulley from Knareborough to York
being 20 Miles
John Burnup from Bentham to York
being 71 Miles
John Bownass from Bentham to York
being 71 Miles'

Both Burnup and Bownass were transported from the magistrate Peter Overend's home in Bentham, which seems to imply they may have been held there after making their respective statements.

The statement by Burnup seems to be the first indication that John Bownass was involved in the murder of Dr Petty. Bownass does not appear to have been a native of Grassington. Conceivably, like Lee, he may have originated from Cumbria before moving to Wharfedale to seek employment in the lead mines. Bownass was certainly a common surname in Cumbria at that point. This may indicate why he was chosen to be Lee's trustworthy partner-in-crime. Perhaps the men even had a history of joint criminal activity before ever moving to the Dales.

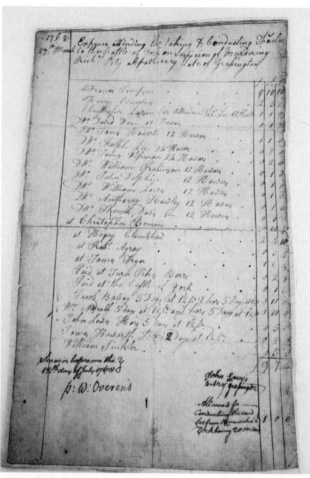

Part of John Petty's accounts relating to the expenses in bringing his
son's killer to justice.
(Courtesy of the Craven Museum)

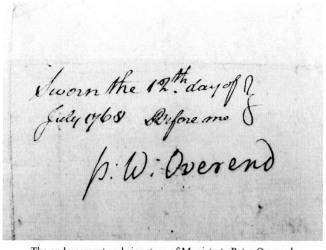

The endorsement and signature of Magistrate Peter Overend
(Courtesy of the Craven Museum)

However, his testimony seems to be a little too convenient. After all, could anyone really recall precisely what they doing, on any given day two years earlier, even to the point of remembering exactly what time they went to bed? The statement was clearly regarded with some suspicion by the magistrate too. It appears that as some point between giving his deposition to Overend and being taken to York, Bownass attempted to leave the scene in a hurry, as the financial accounts of the trial at the Craven Museum show the following payment:

'Upon journey into Derbyshire in search of John Bownass, horse hire and expenses £2 9s 9d' (approximately £500 today)

John Hulley, who was also implicated by Burnup, does not appear to have made an official statement (or, at any rate, if he did, it has not survived). His arrest seems to have been initiated purely on the evidence given by Burnup.

All told, the expenses financed by Richard Petty's father amounted to an initial total of £123 15s and 5d. An additional sum of £9 7s 4d was added later. Presumably these figures (equivalent to approximately £30,000 today) were officially accepted, since they are endorsed as follows:

'Sworn the 12th day
of July 1768 before me
P. W. Overend'

The Next Trial

After all the witnesses had been gathered and the expenses finally paid, it was finally time for the pomp of the Summer Assizes to begin at York, on Saturday 16th July 1768. Both Thomas Lee and his alleged accomplice John Bownass were to finally face trail for the murder of Dr Richard Petty twenty-five months earlier.

John Burnup, who had agreed to turn King's Evidence, was charged separately for his involvement in the tragic affair with the offence of 'assaulting Richard Petty by striking him and thereby causing him a mortal bruise and fracture, of which the said mortal bruise or fracture, Richard Petty then and there instantly died.' No doubt the terrified John Burnup, who displayed an obvious fear of Tom Lee during the trial, hoped that his testimony would ensure a sympathetic hearing.

Before proceeding could begin, a long list of witnesses was read out to those present. These included many of the names listed on the accounts and expenses (mentioned earlier).

List of witnesses at the trial of Thomas Lee

John Burnup	Turned King's Evidence - Statement read in court
Henry Ovington	Landlord of the Angler's Arms at Kilnsey. Testified to Lee's visit with Petty after the Kettlewell cockfight
William Airton	Testified to bringing the body ashore at Litton.
Margaret Calvert	Kettlewell barmaid who testified to seeing Thomas Lee
Thomas Brown	Testified to examining the papers in Dr Petty's waistcoat pocket (in some contemporary reports, he is referred to as Thomas Davis)
Christopher Mitton	Testified to Burnup's conversation with him shortly after the murder
Elizabeth Ellis	Attested to Burnup's presence at Henry Ovington's house in Conistone

Other witnesses were called, such as Isabella Roberts and Mary Ripley, although no record of their evidence survives. Many of the witnesses named in John Petty's accounts and expenses, kept at the Craven Museum, were never in fact called.

The co-conspirators were formally charged for their crimes. Each man's indictment was read separately. Thomas Lee was then brought up to stand in the presence of the Grand Jury,

'Thomas Lee, not having the fear of God before your eyes but being moved and seduced by the instigation of the Devil at the Paish of Burnsall in the County of York, you did feloniously, wilfully, and of malice aforethought make an assault on the head of Richard Petty with great violence, against the Peace of God and our sovereign Lord King.'

It was further added that Dr Petty had been 'choaked and strangled' and that John Bownass and John Hulley had supported Lee in the murder by 'helping abetting comforting assisting and maintaining' him.

This time the Grand Jury decided that the evidence was sufficient for the men to face a trial before a petty (common) jury of twelve men. This was duly arranged for Friday 22nd July 1768. The eminent Mr Justice Joseph Yates would preside. Yates, who had journeyed from his home at Peel Hall in Lancashire for the Assizes, had previously been involved in many high-profile cases of the era, including the trial of Eugene Aram in 1758, the Militia Riots of 1753, and the proceedings against John Wilkes in 1763.

Following the Thomas Lee case, Justice Yates would also rule on the famous copyright case, Millar v Taylor in 1769, before his death one year later at the age of just forty-eight.

Justice Joseph Yates

Returning to Lee's arraignment, the formalities of an eighteenth-century trial continued,

Thomas Lee, hold up thy hand.'

Lee did as he was instructed.

'You stand indicted in the name of Thomas Lee, late of Grassington in the County of York, for the felony of murder. How sayest thou? Art thou guilty of the felony of murder, whereof thou standest, or art thou not guilty?'

Lee answered, 'Not guilty.'

'Culprit, how wilt thou be tried?' asked the Clerk of the Court.

'By God and my country', Lee replied.

John Bownass and Hulley were similarly charged, with both men also pleading 'Not guilty.'

Following an explanation of the crime, John Burnup's statement (which formed the main body of the case against Lee), was read aloud for the jury and transcribed in its entirety in the *Yorkshire Courant* and the *Stamford Mercury* on 28th July (both newspapers incorrectly spelt Burnup as Burnap throughout their coverage of the trial),

'John Burnap, the principal Evidence in this affair, was Servant to Thomas Lee, but left him about two months after the murder was committed, and went into the county of Durham, where on the anniversary of that day two years ago on which Mr Petty was murdered, be mentioned it to his then Master, who took him before a Justice of the Peace, to whom he related the particulars of the murder, whereupon Lee was committed a second time, having been committed on suspicion of the murder in 1766, but no bill could then found against him; however, he now convicted on the following evidence:

John Burnap deposed, that Thomas Lee kept a public house at Grassington, and used to work in the Lead Mines; that he, Burnap, lived as Servant with him; that on Easter Eve, 1766, his Master, John Hully, John Bownass, and himself were in company at his said Master's house that they discoursed about horse stealing and the scarcity of money; that Bownass said it would be no crime to murder somebody and then take his money; that Lee said there would be money enough stirring at Kettlewell Cockings on the Tuesday following, and proposed that the four should go out and rob somebody: that accordingly on Tuesday morning they went to the Cockings, where Lee got into company with Mr. Petty, and it was concerted among them that Hully and Burnap should place themselves at Grass Wood Gate, and bar it with a large stone, to prevent any person passing that way; that Lee and Bownass were to make a noise to apprise Hully and Burnap of their approach. Accordingly, about eight at night, Lee, Bownas, and Petty came together: that Lee, as had been concerted, quarrelled with Petty, or at least pretended to do so, and when he came near the gate gave him a blow on the head with the thick end of his whip; that Hully thereupon came and pulled him off his horse, and held him by the throat till he was dead; that he, Burnap, rifled his pockets, and took thereout three Guineas and two half Guineas, wrapt in an advertisement for Cockings; that they then removed the body, and laid it among some reeds in Grass Wood; after that they removed the body three different times, and lastly, about five weeks after the murder, threw it into the River, and dropped the doctor's gloves by the water side, in order to make be believed he was drowned; that Lee's wife, Bownass, and Hully always assisted in removing the body, and that he, Burnap, was threatened by Hully and Bownass, when Lee was first committed to the Castle, to be served in the same manner that Petty had been, if ever they said anything about it. This evidence, in respect to Mr. Petty's money being wrapt in a printed Bill, and other circumstances, was strongly corroborated by other witnesses.

Lee behaved in the obdurate manner, denying his crime for which he suffered to his last moment.'

It would be another century until an accused person was allowed to speak in their own defence, at trial. The establishment generally believed that most offenders came from the 'criminal classes' and would be likely to prejudice their own case, if given the right to speak, especially as jurors tended to base their verdicts solely on the demeanour and appearance of the defendant. There is no surviving record of any defence being offered by Lee (other than his plea of 'not guilty'). Neither was Jane Lee permitted to testify, either for or against her husband, under the ancient common law of spousal privilege.

With the evidence now heard, it was time for the jury to consider their verdict. At most eighteenth-century Assize sessions, there was a deliberate time pressure placed on jurors to 'encourage' a hasty decision. Many cases were expected to be heard in a just a few days, therefore speed was of the essence. While today, a murder trial may last several days or weeks, three centuries ago they seldom exceeded a few hours. Jurors were usually goaded into a small, uncomfortable, and unheated room – 'without meat, drink, fire, or candle' – and the course of justice was expected to race to a speedy conclusion.

Mr Justice Yates was, no doubt, expected at another Assize session elsewhere and would be impatient in the hope of a timely verdict.

A few minutes later the jury returned to be addressed by the Clerk of Arraigns,

'Look upon the prisoner, Gentleman of the Jury. How say you? Is Thomas Lee guilty of the felony of murder or which he stands indicted, or not guilty?'

'Guilty of murder.'

Thomas Lee was sentenced to death by Mr Justice Yates and the following entry recorded in the Gaol Book at York Castle,

'Thomas Lee. Attainted of murder – To be hanged on Monday the 25th day of July instant and his body to be dissected and anatomised.'

The *Murder Act 1752* allowed for a post-mortem dissection of the executed criminal. The *Act* stated that the bodies of criminals would be given to a surgeon, as directed by the judge, and even provided a clause to protect against the family's attempts to reclaim the body.

Although the *Murder Act* provided medical science with much needed cadavers, it was primarily intended as a punitive measure. The preamble to the *Act* pointed out the necessity for some 'further terror and peculiar mark of infamy' to be included as part of the death penalty. The measure was believed to have acted as a useful deterrent, with the families of the executed man often more preoccupied with the fate of the body rather than the hanging itself. Indeed, in 1829, Sir Walter Scott commented that dissection as a punishment was an effective one, 'criminals have been known to shrink from that part of the sentence which seems to affect them more than the doom of death itself.'

Accordingly, in the margin of the York Castle Gaol Book, next to the sentencing of Thomas Lee, is written,

'Let the body of Thomas Lee after execution be hung in chains as near as may be convenient to Grassington Gate near the town of Grassington.'

Lee's accomplice, John Hulley and John Bownass were acquitted. The *Manchester Mercury*, in its edition of the 2nd August 1768 pointed out that, 'the men ever ought to be thankful for a humane jury.'

John Burnup, in light of his crucial evidence, was 'discharged by proclamation' and walked free.

Thomas Lee was not so lucky. Again, the *Manchester Mercury* recorded the following,

'The Assizes ended here at the Crown End, when Thomas Lee, attainted of murder, received sentence of death, and was executed at Tyburn yesterday, the 25th day of July 1768.'

Returning to the verdict, Thomas Lee was effectively condemned purely on the weight of John Burnup's statement. Although several witnesses corroborated parts of Burnup's evidence – mainly, that they too had seen Lee and Dr Petty travelling between Kettlewell Cockings and Grassington – his conviction was largely circumstantial by today's standards. However, in an era before the advent of fingerprints, DNA, and CCTV, unless the murderer was caught with a bloody knife in hand, the majority of convictions tended to be solely based on eyewitness testimony.

Thomas Lee was publicly hanged on Monday 25th July 1768, at the York gallows at Knavesmire, close to Micklegate Bar at the, then, outskirts of the city. The execution site was commonly known as York Tyburn, after the original Tyburn gallows in Middlesex. Originally erected in 1379 the gallows had been the scene of many gruesome executions, including the hanging of infamous highwayman Dick Turpin in 1739.

The Catholic priests Alexander Rawlins and Henry Walpole were hanged, drawn and quartered there in 1595, twenty-two Jacobite rebels were hanged at Tyburn following the '45 rebellion, and Elizabeth Broadingham was burned at the stake there in 1790 for the murder of her husband.

However, by the beginning of the nineteenth century, it was felt that the gallows did not create a good first impression for the many wealthy visitors entering York to transact their business. As a result, the last hanging at Knavesmire took place in 1801, after which the gallows were moved to a more discreet location close to York Castle. Today, a small, paved area with a commemorative plaque marks the position in which the wooden scaffold once stood.

It is not known how many people gathered to watch Lee's execution, however, public executions were generally well attended. The records of the prison at York Castle lists simply that,

'Hanged, Thomas Lee, Highway robber, for the murder of Richard Petty at Burnsall on 1 Apr 1766. His body hung in chains at Grassington Gate, Grassington.'

The execution was then publicly announced in the *St James Chronicle* and the *Public Advertiser*; a tactic used by the authorities to heap further shame on the families.

As mentioned above, the practice of then displaying the executed man's body at the scene of his crime was undertaken with some relish. This gruesome procedure served as a stark deterrent to those considering a life of crime. Lee's limp corpse was subsequently taken from the gallows and conveyed the forty-five miles to Grassington by horse and cart. The sombre party breaking the journey with an overnight stop at the Blue Bell Inn in Knaresborough High Street. A 'posting house', the Blue Bell Inn provided overnight accommodation for travellers and stabling for horses. Although now largely rebuilt, the inn still exists as The Crown. Displayed inside you will find lots of interesting information regarding the Inn's history.

Some documentary evidence still survives to highlight the details of Lee's macabre journey to Grassington. It is recalled in Norrison Scatcherd's *Gleanings after Eugene Aram*, published in 1836, that Ann Aram (who had lived on the High Street on as a child) watched the procession arrive,

'When Thomas Lee, the noted highwayman, was brought through Knaresborough, preparatory to being hung in chains at Grassington, the procession stopped for the night at the Blue Bell Inn where he was put into a stable for the night. A great mob assembled to see his body depart.'

However, before the body of Thomas Lee could be gibbeted and displayed at the entrance to Grassington Wood (or at the Grassington Gate, near the bridge. There seems to be conflicting evidence pointing to either alternative), the gruesome process of constructing a gibbet cage was required. A local blacksmith was usually commissioned to build an iron cage, designed to house the body in an upright position from the gallows, or gibbet. Gibbet cages were expensive to produce, as the size of each victim varied. Every cage was required to suspend the corpse in an upright fashion. Once the body began to decompose, the cage would be expected to keep the limbs attached to the body for as long as possible, often years. The wooden gibbets, from which the body was then suspended, needed to be sturdy structures, capable of standing for decades, with the bodies that dangled and swayed from them slowly decaying into skeletons over long periods of time. Many gibbets stood more than thirty-feet tall and included obstacles designed to prevent the executed man's loved ones from removing the corpse, in the hope of alleviating the family's disgrace.

The gibbet served three purposes; it allowed for the hanged man's punishment to continue, even after death. The slowly decomposing corpse also helped to heap yet more shame on the victim's family, as well as serving as a clear warning to any other would-be criminals.

The practice of gibbeting had first developed during the medieval period, and reached its peak in England during the 1740s. As mentioned earlier, the *Murder Act 1752* required that all bodies belonging to criminals must either be publicly gibbeted or dissected.

Returning to July 1768, the body of Thomas Lee made its way in procession towards the scene of his crime two years earlier. Writing in 1869, the Rev Bailey John Harker wrote in *Rambles in Upper Wharfedale,*

'It must have been an awful time for his wife and relatives; when his body was brought to Grassington, hundreds of people flocked to see it, and from there they followed it to the place where the last penalty of national law was carried out, and where it hung till it dropped all together, a ghastly sight and warning to all passers-by. It is said that gypsies stole the buckles from his shoes, and that in the night time his ghost wanders through the wood, telling its guilt to the winds.'

Rev. Bailey Harker

The Rev Harker was clearly troubled by the death of Dr Petty, since he referred to it again in *Philip Neville of Garriton: A Yorkshire Tale*, published in 1875,

'Near where the murder was committed, close by the highway that leads through the wood, the body of the murderer, as a warning to passers-by, hung, a ghastly object....the bones being carried away by gypsies and sold at the rag stores.'

Whilst a Romany tradition did exist, in which the bones and trinkets from a corpse were considered lucky, there is no direct evidence to link their theft to any passing travellers. In reality, the elegant stockings, buckles, and shoes said to have been worn by Thomas Lee, may have been stolen by anyone, even the men charged with placing his body inside the gibbet.

Thomas Lee's body is believed to have remained suspended in the gibbet cage for a number of years, probably on a small hillock (sometimes known as Lee's Hill), at the entrance to Grassington Wood. Birds would have no doubt pecked the decomposing flesh from the corpse, leaving bleached white bones to fall to the ground only to be carried away by scavenging animals or gruesome souvenir hunters. Joseph Robertshaw (writing a century later) certainly believed that Lee's body stayed on its gibbet in Grassington Wood for at least four years. The general practice was to allow the body to remain in situ until only the skeleton remained, although English history is full of infamous examples in which decomposing corpses hung for as long as a decade.

There is another version of the story, in which Lee's gibbet was erected at the entrance into Grassington, near the bridge, where the current 'Welcome to Grassington' sign now stands. There would certainly be valid reasons for placing it there, however, the greater weight of evidence suggests it was situated at the entrance into Grass Wood.

Finally, when Lee's remains had all but disappeared, the gibbet irons were removed and thrown into the River Wharfe, eventually snagging at a point near Ghaistrills Strid (a narrow rocky stretch of the Wharfe close to Grass Wood), as they made their way downstream. From here, the irons were taken to a spot on the river further downstream at Tom Crag and hurled in once more.

It then appears that a group of boys, playing one Sunday morning before church, retrieved the gibbet irons and hung them from a tree near to the end of Grassington Bridge. The boys intended to exhibit the irons through the streets of the town (no doubt to earn some rather dubious pocket money); however, a group of townsfolk on their way to church interfered, removing the irons and then secretly burying them the following morning, in a field close to the east end of the bridge. There is no precise date attached to this part of the story, although the bridge over the Wharfe at Grassington has been in existence since the mid-seventeenth century, meaning there is no reason to doubt the story's validity. The bridge was widened in 1780 and a substantial amount of strengthening work undertaken, mainly to help support the extra weight of traffic caused by the increasing number of horse and carts journeying back and forth from the lead mines. It is feasible - if this part of Thomas Lee's story is indeed true – that the irons may have been disturbed and surfaced around 1780, as a result of work being carried out to the bridge supports.

We do know that the irons then remained undisturbed for many years, probably until the early 1860s, when they were witnessed by the Rev. Harker. Born in 1844 in Grassington, Harker would have only been a young man at the time, and seeing the rusty gibbet irons clearly made an impression on him. He referred to the incident in his 1890 book *The Buxton of Yorkshire*, in which he states that the artifacts had originally been seized from the enterprising boys by a descendant of Thomas Lee's and then buried in a nearby field. The irons were then unearthed during the digging of a pit, in which it had been planned to bury a dead cow.

That seems to be the last known thread of evidence in the search for the gibbet irons. They were taken into the possession of another party and their whereabouts is now unknown.

Rev. Harker lived until 1916, at which time he passed away in Grassington at the age of 72. He does not appear to have shed any further light on the location of Lee's gibbet irons.

Other writers have also theorised regarding the final location of Lee's irons. John Crowther mentions the events in his 1930 guide to the area, *Silva Garrs (Grass Wood)*, in which he explains that the body of Thomas Lee was hung on a wooden gibbet atop a mound overlooking the scene of his crime, and that the irons were eventually buried in Donkey Field, close to Grassington Bridge. Many years later, according to Crowther's account, several Grassington residents were digging a pit in the field, in which to bury a cow, and accidentally unearthed the remains of the gibbet cage and irons. They chose to leave them in situ, where they still remain.

It is claimed that Thomas Lee was the last murderer in Wharfedale to suffer the barbaric indignity of gibbeting. Although the practice was not finally abolished until the passing of the Anatomy Act 1834 (sixty-eight years after Lee's execution), in truth, the punishment had mostly fallen out of favour even by 1768.

The dubious honour of being the final murderers in England to have their bodies publicly gibbeted fell to a Jarrow miner, William Jobling, and a Leicester bookbinder, James Cook. Both men's bodies suffered this ignominious end in 1832. Contemporary descriptions of their fate do provide us with a valuable and graphic insight into the procedure and the probable fate of Thomas Lee's body,

'The body was encased in flat bars of iron of two and a half inches in breadth, the feet were placed in stirrups, from which a bar of iron went up each side of the head, and ended in a ring by which he was suspended; a bar from the collar went down the breast, and another down the back, there were also bars in the inside of the legs which communicated with the above; and crossbars at the ankles, the knees, the thighs, the bowels, the breast and the shoulders; the hands were hung by the side and covered with pitch, the face was pitched and covered with a piece of white cloth.'

(Description of William Jobling's fate from *The Local Historian's Table Book connected with the Counties of Newcastle-upon-Tyne, Northumberland and Durham* (1844) by Moses Richardson)

'The head was shaved and tarred, to preserve it from the action of the weather; and the cap in which he had suffered was drawn over his face. On Saturday afternoon his body, attired as at the time of his execution, having been firmly fixed in the irons necessary to keep the limbs together, was carried to the place of its intended suspension.

Thousands of persons were attracted to the spot, to view this novel but most barbarous exhibition; and considerable annoyance was felt by persons resident in the neighbourhood of the dreadful scene.'

(The Newgate Calendar 1832)

The Legacy of Thomas Lee

The story of Thomas Lee does not end there. Almost inevitably, the gruesome tale soon became one of Yorkshire legend and attracted many embellishments and convenient coincidences.

With the advent of the railways and the growth in tourism during the Victorian era, the story would soon become the legend known today as the 'Heather Bell' version, written by Joseph Robertshaw during the 1850s. Over time, this has evolved into the accepted version of events. Perhaps the only thing missing from the saga of Dr Petty's murder was a good old-fashioned ghost story. Almost inevitably, this would soon follow.

The stretch of the River Wharfe adjoining Grass Wood, and chosen by Lee as the spot in which to kill the doctor, is known locally as the Ghaisthylls. At the time of Dr Petty's murder, it was a quiet spot, seldom visited, and heaped in superstition; mostly due to the number of local inhabitants who had accidently drowned there. In an edition of the *Craven Herald* from February 1856, Dr Dixon refers to the hauntings in Grass Wood,

'Tom Lee who was gibbeted in it, often comes again; aye! And so does the man he murdered!'

Grass Wood

In the following month's issue, Daniel Cooper also records an encounter in Grass Wood, in which he recounts his story to the fictional character Captain Trenoodle,

'I now walked on leisurely, and soon arrived at Tom Lee's gibbet – it's fallen down now, perhaps been carried away; but then it was standing, and a few of the murderer's bones, blanched by the weather, presented an awful and disgusting object. I had often passed the gibbet without feeling the least fear; but on this evening . . . I was ill at ease.'

The story takes an interesting twist when Daniel Cooper meets an old man, dressed in an old-fashioned waistcoat and breeches, and carrying a gold-tipped cane. While the two men walk on together it becomes apparent that the old man is in fact a spectral manifestation of Dr Petty. Clearly, for the purposes of this tale and contrary to tradition, ghosts are able to age!

Rev. Harker (as mentioned earlier), referred to the story of Tom Lee in *Philip Neville of Garriton: A Yorkshire Tale* in 1875. The book also mentions the legend of Lee's ghost,

'I've nivver seen it. I've come through t'wood nearly all times at night, but I neither seen nor heard owt.'

Perhaps the most widely heard reference to the existence of a ghost in Grass Wood, came on Thursday 19th November 1936, when BBC Radio broadcast a live play called 'The Ghost of Grassington' on its Northern Programme. Due to its murderous content, the play was not broadcast until 9.05pm, and was sandwiched between a pianoforte recital by Frederick Dawson and the BBC news. Nevertheless, it reached tens of thousands of listeners, bringing the story of Tom Lee to a new generation.

Radio :

A DRAMATIC re-construction of the story of " The Ghost of Grassington," will be broadcast to Northern listeners to-night. The play has been written by " Diana Dale "—the pen-name of a new radio-dramatist from Ben Rhydding, Yorkshire. Grass Wood, on the lonely road between Grassington and Kilnsey, in Wharfedale, is the scene of the ghostly visitations; for it is there, so the story goes, that the village doctor was foully done to death towards the end of the 18th century.

NORTHERN PROGRAMME (449.1m., 668kc'

5.15.—Children's Hour.

6. 0.—The Black Dyke Mills Band; conductor, Arthur O. Pearce; Albert Murgatroyd (baritone).

7. 0.—Second News, Weather.

7.20.—Northern Announcements; Bulletin for Farmers.

7.30.—The Alfredo Campoli Trio.

7.55.—Introduction to " Madam Butterfly."

8. 0.—" Madam Butterfly " (Puccini) (Act 1); produced by John B. Gordon. with Tudor Davies, Powell Lloyd, Rose Morris, Sumner Austin, Joan Cross, John Greenwood, Frank Brooke, Harry Brindle, Rosina Tanner, Rose Carlton; conductor, Lawrance Collingwood; Chorus Master, Geoffrey Corbett, from Sadler's Wells Theatre.

8.45.—A Pianoforte Recital by Frederick Dawson.

9. 5.—" The Ghost of Grassington," by Diana Dale; produced by Jan Bussell, with H. C. Rycroft, E. Parsons, Roni Vine. C. B. Pulman, Ian Baldwin, F. J. O. Coddington, F. A. Bean, J. R. Phillips, Mary Wilkinson, Frank Crosland, Philip Robinson and James Harrison.

10.0.—News Summary, Weather, Sport, Topical Talks.

Even in the twenty-first century the story of Tom Lee's phantom spirit continues to fascinate the modern generation of ghosthunters. The UK Haunted Locations Database website features the legend of Tom Lee and even displays a handy GPS map location for any would-be spectral seeker,

'In Gibbet hill in Grass Wood, near Upper Wharfedale, piercing cries of anger and pain can sometimes be heard and occasionally, the figure of a man with an evil face uttering curses can be glimpsed (some reports say that a screaming, floating skull is sometimes seen). Tom Lee was a blacksmith many years ago but turned to the more lucrative occupation of highway robbery. During one escapade he was wounded and sought medical help. As he was being tended the doctor made it be known that he knew how he had acquired the injury and Tom agreed to end his activities if the authorities were not informed. However, Tom felt confined by this agreement and murdered the doctor in Grassington Wood as he returned home one night.'

In recent years, the Leeds-List website has also featured the story of Tom Lee in an article showcasing Yorkshire's most famous ghost legends,

'The Yorkshire Dales market town of Grassington was the unlikely location of a murder in the 18th century and it still haunts the area to this day. The grizzly event took place back in 1766, when local blacksmith Tom Lee shot and killed Dr Richard Petty after a cock fight where the doctor won a substantial amount of money. Lee hid out in a nearby cave – and spookily enough, his ghost is said to still call it home.

Lee was originally acquitted of the murder but later re-tried and hanged at York. His body was left suspended at Grass Wood in an iron gibbet until it decomposed and the bones fell to the ground. Not surprisingly, Lee's ghost is said to roam Grass Wood to this day – be careful if you ever visit.'

Once the dust had settled following Lee's execution, and the gibbet removed, the town of Grassington returned to normal. Jane Lee remained in Grassington, passing away in 1777. She was buried at St Michael's Church in Linton, alongside her mother who had died three years earlier. Lee's youngest child, Thomas (junior) married Margaret Ashbrough at the same church in 1789, aged twenty-two. He passed away in 1815 and was also interred at St Michael's. Lee's daughter Mary married a man named James Rodgers in 1775, aged twenty, and lived to the ripe old age of ninety-one. There is little record of the Lee's other daughter, Elizabeth, other than that of her baptism at St Michael's in 1861, although it is possible that she passed away as a child.

There are not thought to be any descendants of Tom Lee now living in the area.

There are no records to indicate that Dr Richard Petty was married, however, the surname is still a common one in the Colne and Craven area. Many of these may be descended from Richard Petty's nephews, Edward and Richard (junior), both of whom were also doctors. Interestingly, Dr Petty's murder in Grass Wood was not the only violent death suffered by a member of the Petty family. In 1825, the *Leeds Mercury* reported the following tragic story,

'A melancholy accident happened in the neighbourhood of Colne on Wednesday last (7th December 1825). It appears that Mr Petty, Surgeon and Apothecary of Colne, had been called in the course of the day professionally to Barnoldswick in Craven, where he was detained until evening, and that on his return home, along the banks of the Leeds and Liverpool Canal, in riding under one of the bridges, he had fallen from his horse, and was precipitated into the water, where he was found about eight o'clock at night, by a number of work-people, a lifeless corpse, with his horse still standing on the bank.'

The legend of Thomas Petty and the brutal murder of Dr Petty has now become entrenched in Wharfedale folklore, largely thanks to the version of events published by Joseph Robertshaw in the 1850s, under the pseudonym 'Heather Bell'. This re-imagining of the story forms the second half of this book, allowing the reader the opportunity to contrast the known facts with the romanticised Victorian version, written for the newly burgeoning tourist market.

However, before we examine the 'Heather Bell' story in detail, it is also worthwhile noting that a slightly different variation of the Tom Lee story appeared in the *Yorkshire Gazette* in 1901, as part of a series entitled *Famous Yorkshire Trials*. This version features one or two deviations from the more accepted plot.

'FAMOUS YORKSHIRE TRIALS - THE GRASSINGTON MURDER (1901 VERSION)

The story of this crime lives in the Skipton district still, and old folks at Grassington and Kilnsey will tell you with awe of Tom Lee and his dreadful deed.

More than a hundred years have passed since Lee was the landlord of one of the Grassington Inns. He was a man of immense strength, and was the terror of the neighbourhood. He was a poacher, and at times went further and played the highwayman to some profit.

There were some lead mines at Grassington which belonged to Dr Petty, a resident there, and one day, having disguised himself, Lee waylaid, in broad daylight, the Doctor's agent as he was making his way on horseback from Green Hill to Grassington, with a lot of money for the wages in his possession.

Of this encounter Lee got much the worst, and was in the end glad to escape with just a nasty pistol wound. Then came trouble. The only doctor in the district was the man whose property he had tried to take by force, and yet, undaunted, Lee made his way to Dr Petty and was compelled to admit his guilt. Highway robbery was a hanging matter in those days, but the doctor let no one into the great secret. He would have been wise had he been less kind, and had handed Lee, there and then, over to the gallows.

Things might have rested in this way had the doctor realised the perilous nature of his secret. But one day he stopped on his rounds at the Anglers' Inn at Kilnsey where Lee was engaged in a violent quarrel with a young farmer, and to silence Lee, let drop a mysterious hint. The doctor shortly afterwards left, and tradition has it that when he had drained the stirrup cup, which the landlord handed to him, he let the glass fall, and, to the horror of all, it did not break. In that countryside this is always taken for a presage of terrible evil.

While on his homeward journey through Grass Wood, the doctor's horse shied, and the same moment a heavy hand grasped the poor gentleman and dragged him to the ground.

The terrible story which follows we are able to give from Lee's confession. The doctor recognised his assailant, and struggled for his life, but Lee, owing to his superior strength, quickly got the mastery, and twice stabbed the prostrate man. Then he dragged the body beneath the shadow of a near wall, and covered it over with grass and weeds.

Perhaps the most dramatic part of the story is yet to come. Lee made his way home. The Inn was of course at this late hour closed, and his wife got up from bed to let him in. The mere sight of his face told her that it had been no mere poaching affair which he had been engaged in; so, once up in the bedroom, the woman put question after question to elicit the secret.

As Lee stated subsequently, he knew that he should want help in the better secreting of his victim's body, and so at last he told her.

For a moment her hand went to her heart in horror, and then she seemed to realise to the full the danger which threatened him, and there and then, with bated breath, the two of them, in that still house, discussed plan after plan for the hiding of the body.

Suddenly his wife stopped dead. "Hush!" she said, in an awful whisper, "Tom Bowness may have heard!" Tom Lee was up in a moment, and at once went stealthily to see whether the apprentice was asleep or not.

The lad had heard all, but pretended to be asleep. When, however, his master, knife in hand, crept nearer to his bed, the horror of it all was too much for him, and he sprang up in his bed half mad with terror. Lee seized him by the throat. "Oh, spare my life," implored the lad. "What has thoo heerd?" Tom asked. "I've not heerd at all, Tom. I'm sure I hevvant," gasped the lad.

For a moment it seemed as if the man was about to commit a second murder; but an idea occurred to him.

"Put on your clothes," he said, and the lad did so, and shortly after the two set out, Tom with a large sack over his arm, and made their way to Grass Wood. The idea was to secure the lad's silence by implicating him in the removal of the body to a securer hiding place.

But when they reached the spot they found to their horror that the doctor was not dead. There, in the darkness, they found him helplessly crawling over the mould, and crying, with a weak voice, for aid. The bare sight would have wrought almost the hardest heart to pity, but it only hardened Lee. Under the threat of instant murder, he compelled his now hopelessly involved apprentice to finish the work with a stake. Then they put the body into a sack, and carrying it up to the rocky ground above, succeeded, as they thought, in finding a safe burying-place.

Long before this the poor doctor's riderless horse had made his way home. Unfortunately, however, this caused surprise instead of alarm. It was believed that the doctor had been detained at some patient's house and the animal had broken loose from his tethering. So, Mrs Petty and servant waited up all night. When the morning brought neither man nor message, surprise gave way to alarm, and very soon did all Grassington know that Dr Petty had mysteriously disappeared. The missing man was easily traced to the Anglers' Inn at Kilnsey, but the rest of his journey was mere surmise, so search parties were organised.

It was, of course, only a question of hours before searchers had come across the spot in Grass Wood, with all its terrible signs of a struggle, and then at once the worst was feared. When people, too, remembered the incident at the Anglers' Inn, where the Doctor and Lee had words together, Lee's name was at once associated with the supposed crime in a way which alarmed him.

Naturally Lee anticipated that a strict search would be made for the body, and so that night, when the startled villagers were sleeping, he set out with the servant lad once more. This time they took Lee's pony with them, and swinging the horrible sack over his saddle, they made for a boggy part of the moorland beyond the wood and then breathed again. Lee believed that his secret was now safe for ever.

After this, several weeks elapsed without anything further being done. There was not the police system in those days which we have now, and the villagers satisfied themselves with talking; and Lee had never cared much what had been said of him. He was, however, seriously alarmed when he heard it whispered that an old farmer had seen him and his pony on the moorland on that fateful night, so he waited for a time when there was no moon, and, with his wite this time, set out once again. Once more they dug up the body and placed it on the pony's back, and passed over the moor towards Hebden and on to Burnsall, and there, tying a stone to the sack, they rolled it into the river.

There were, however, clearly seen this time by a young man who had been visiting his sweetheart, and when the sack was removed from the water there was such excitement in the whole district as had never been known before.

The legal proceedings which followed were characteristic of those times. Lee was at once arrested on the coroner's warrant, but the scant evidence which could be procured did not amount to proof that he had committed the murder, and the jury acquitted him.

As he was hurrying home in a high state of elation, he was arrested again on a magistrate's warrant. Remand followed remand, and yet once again, after a most searching examination, Lee was acquitted for the second time.

Three years passed away, and still the man was at large, and now more than ever the terror of the neighbourhood. One morning, to his great alarm, he was arrested for the third time, and, carefully guarded, the officers took him to York Castle. Lee's newly-awakened fears settled down to despair. He soon learnt that Bownass, his apprentice, under the strings of conscience had turned King's evidence, and Lee knew that the missing links in the chain of evidence would now be supplied. This time he was immediately convicted, was executed at Tyburn, and

swung from a gibbet for four years afterwards in Grass Wood – the scene of his terrible crime.'
(YORKSHIRE GAZETTE 9 March 1901)

Before we begin the colourful Victorian version of the Tom Lee story, it is also worth mentioning another murder which Lee, it seems, was almost certainly involved in.

Allanson Skaife, son of Thomas Skaife, a wealthy gentleman from Ripon, was robbed and murdered on Sawley Moor on 23rd February 1765. Skaife was returning to the family home in Ripon at the time. In the first of many similarities with the modus operandi of Tom Lee, Allanson had been collecting rents from tenants at Littlethorpe, and was riding home when he was waylaid, murdered, and robbed of all valuables, with the exception of his silver buckles. His horse returned riderless to Braisty Woods, which caused his family to raise the alarm. A search party was hastily organised, which resulted in the body being discovered soon afterwards. Allanson Skaife was buried at St Jude's Church in Hartwith, near Harrogate.

Although not recorded in the reported evidence at Tom Lee's later trial for the murder of Dr Petty, it was a firmly held belief among the descendants of Mr Allanson Skaife that John Burnup had also confessed that he had been Lee's accomplice, one year earlier, in the murder of their unfortunate ancestor.

This information has remained a long-held tradition in the Skaife family, and was recorded by William Grainge in his memoir *Nidderdale*, written in 1863, and based on his conversations with Mr R. D. Skaife of York.

Perhaps this is yet more evidence that *The Grassington Murder* should have been titled *The Grassington Serial Killer.*

PART TWO:

Tom Lee: A Wharfedale Tragedy

by 'Heather Bell' (Joseph Robertshaw), Originally Published 1862. Edited and annotated by Mark Bridgeman

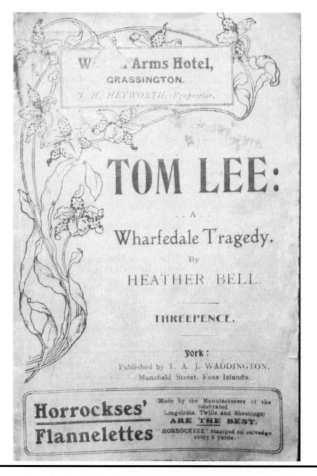

The unfolding story of Tom Lee begins in chapter two of Joseph Robertshaw's 1862 book (which was part travelogue). Aside from correcting the many printing errors and 'typos' within the original manuscript, I have faithfully reproduced the tale in its entirety. As mentioned in my introduction, Robertshaw's version of events was created for the Victorian literature and tourist market. The language is understandably romanticised, flowery, and drenched in colloquialisms, which I hope the reader will view with interest and sympathy. It offers a fascinating window into the writing and culture of the period. I have made some minor changes and edits where the author's original meaning is confusing or lost, and slightly diluted some of Robertshaw's attempts to mimic the regional accent which occasionally makes the text almost impossible to understand. Nevertheless, I have left all the delightful and archaic Victorian words and phrases intact. There is a unique pleasure in unearthing their meaning for yourself.

The story of Tom Lee: A Wharfedale Tragedy begins in chapter two of Robertshaw's book, following a tour through the region:

Chapter II   The Stirrup Cup

"On the afternoon of a certain day, somewhere about ninety years ago, and towards the close of the year, a horseman might have been seen cantering along the road leading from Grassington to Coniston. He was a middle-aged man, of respectable appearance, and one upon whom the cares of life seemed to sit lightly. He was of a ruddy complexion – had sharp features and iron-grey hair, a restless piercing eye, whose expression indicated that at times its possessor delighted to indulge in a little mischievous fun at the expense of others, but the general expression of his features wore an easy gentlemanly aspect, which bespoke a man in easy circumstances, and at peace with both himself and all the world.

His appearance denoted the professional man; and such was the case, for he practiced the healing art among the inhabitants of the district, and was very well liked in the neighbourhood.

Among a scattered population, persons in his capacity have frequently a pretty long distance to go to visit their patients, and on the present occasion he was taking one of his accustomed rounds. After calling at Coniston, he pursued his way over the bridge at the foot of the hill in the direction of Kilnsey, and on reaching the village he put up his horse, as was sometimes his custom when he had a few patients to visit there, at the Angler's Inn. As the doctor rode up to the door 'mine host' was standing there, and accosted him with,

"How d'ye do, Mr Petty? A sharp wind this afternoon."
"Very keen, Landlord, for the season. Whom have you inside?" asked the doctor, hearing a loud conversation in the kitchen.
"It's Tom Lee and Dick Linton. They can't see things in the same light altogether – got rather across. That Tom Lee is as noisy and contrary when he's had a drop o' drink, as he's glum and peevish at other times."

"Oh, it's Tom is it. He Likes to be spouting vinegar, does Tom; he's a rum customer," said the doctor, as he handed the reins to Boniface; "put up my horse, will you?" added he as he started down the village street.

"What, aren't ye going to call?" asked the landlord.

"Yes, yes," answered Petty, "as I come up. I shan't be long before I'm back. I must crack a joke or two with Tom," added he, laughing and proceeding on his way.

"Whose horse is that?" asked Dame Hodgson, just then coming to the door.

"It's Petty's. He's calling for a short time when's he's done his business.

"Oh, then we must get the parlour ready for him?" said she inquiringly.

"It's no use, he'll be for th' kitchen by what he said," shouted her spouse as he led off the horse into the backyard.

Meanwhile the parties in the kitchen carried on their noisy conversation, which every now and then threatened to terminate in fisticuffs, which catastrophe the good dame managed to ward off by adroitly putting in a mollifying word or two, thereby pacifying for a short time the wordy belligerents. After a short cessation, Dick Linton, who was a small farmer in that neighbourhood, but being fonder of his glass than minding his business, was only therefore in poor circumstances, again broke out –

"It caps the world, Tom, it does; I connect tell how tha' manages it. I'm nowt to crack on, and for ought I know, I work as hard as thee; but well I'm as poor as a nit, thou's always plenty o' brass to sit on. How is that – con ye tell me that bit?"

"What's that to thee, thou flutter-muck?" growled Tom, "it'll happen it's as well for thee to mind thy own business: if thou doesn't I can straighten off wi' thee; by hook or crook."

The person who gave this answer sat on one side of the fire of an old-fashioned long settle. At a little distance from him, on a deal table whose top was scoured till it was white as driven snow, stood the pewter quart out of which he took every now and then a deep potation. He was a tall, sinewy individual, rather round shouldered, and though not stout, was of that tough, wiry build that few persons would have had much chance of overpowering him in a trial of strength. He was not only strong in frame, but he had a dark vindictive spirit; cunning and revengeful, he seldom wavered in his purposes; for once bent upon the accomplishment of an object, he generally found means, sooner or later, to carry out his designs.

His disposition and personal strength being well known far and wide, he was the dread of the whole district, and very few had the hardihood to interfere with him in any of his proceedings. Moreover, burglaries were no uncommon events in those parts; so far from being so, they happened so frequently that the inhabitants became quite alarmed, and made their properties as secure from depredations as they possibly could. The name of Tom Lee was freely handed about, in a quiet way, amongst a great many persons, as there was considerable suspicion felt by them, that its owner had to do with many, if not all, the depredations that were committed from time to time in the neighbourhood.

Indeed, with some it was not mere suspicion, but a certain knowledge that he was implicated in those burglaries; but a fear of raising his revengeful ire against them sealed their lips. Precaution, as we have just said, led them to take measures to guard their dwellings against his effect an entrance, and to this day are to be found strong iron bars in the wide, old-fashioned chimneys of several farm houses, placed there to prevent Tom's midnight visits; for it was in this way that he generally made his ingress into the homesteads of the honest farmers. But he was not always successful in his midnight maraudings; so far from this, he not only failed frequently in gaining his points, but on more than one occasion he was roughly handled by parties that he little thought were prepared for his attacks. Many a gunshot wound did he receive; but the persons who thus repulsed him did it in ambuscade, and so long as he knew not who they were, they contented themselves with his mode of chastisement, rather than push matters to the law; and this mode of foiling Tom exasperated him far more than taking the other course, for he did not know upon whom to wreak his vengeance. In these cases he had a great deal of suffering, for he had to get his wounds healed again privately as best he could not daring to go to any Leech, for fear of effect being traced up to its cause. On one occasion, however, the wound he received was of such a nature that he was compelled to seek the advice of the village doctor, Dr Petty, for his life was greatly jeopardised. In connection with the then extensive lead mines of this district, the wages of the workmen were paid fortnightly, and a person from Green Hill – another village father up the Dales where was another extensive mine belonging to the same company – was accustomed to bring down to Grassington the cash for wages in bags, and which amounted to a good round sum. Tom, of course, knew of this, and in thinking about it as he frequently did, his cupidity was excited – his fingers edged to get hold of the bags, and he determined to possess himself of them for once if he possibly could.

The design was no sooner formed then he set about carrying it out, by waylaying the person who rode down from Greenhill with the money, and, by overpowering him, secure the booty. One great obstacle to his accomplishing this was, it would have to be done during daylight; but by disguising himself, and making the attack on the most unfrequented part of the road, he hoped to succeed. The opportunity at length came, he mounted his horse (for he kept a horse of his own) and repaired to the spot he had marked out for the attack, but thanks to the vigilance of the money carrier, he eluded Toms first onset, and putting spurs to his horse, got the lead a little distance. Tom was not long, however, before he came up with him, and was just about striking him a heavy blow with a bludgeon he had provided himself with for the purpose, when the miner, driven to such an extremity, drew forth a pistol and lodged a quantity of shot in that part of Tom's person which was covered by the upper part of his leathern breaches.

This brought him to a stand; and (while the miner galloped off rejoicing in his deliverance from the clutches of the unknown assailant, and mightily pleased at the thought of having so well peppered him) he slowly rode along a bye-path, which led to a lonely place among some weather-beaten rocks on the moorlands above. There he remained in the greatest agony till the shades of night covered his retreat to Grassington. His wounds were so dangerous, and the pain so excruciating, he was under the necessity of calling in the assistance of Petty. The news had already got noised through the village, of the miner having been attacked, and of course the doctor once identified Tom as the person who had made it, but at his patient's earnest entreaty hushed the matter up. Under the doctor's hands Tom ultimately recovered, and though many suspected him of being concerned in the affair, yet no one dared to charge him with it, and in the course of time it was forgotten as the minds of the villagers were taken up with succeeding seven days' wonders. The doctor however, would occasionally revert to it, to the no small mortification of Tom, and he began to dislike the doctor, not from any personal bad feeling, but because he felt he was in the doctor's power and sometimes he felt insecure.

This feeling of insecurity had more than once started a thought in Tom's mind which at length began to take the shape of a deliberate purpose, and that was to take the doctor's life. Tom resided at Grassington, and, as we have before said, kept an inn he did not pay much attention to his business, however, but left it mainly in the care of an apprentice there, but by trade he was a blacksmith. "Like master like man," as the old adage hath it. The business did not succeed under the management of Jack Sharp, for Jack had got into the same loose, careless way that his master was in, and not infrequently had he to assist Tom in his secret, nefarious practises.

Search was Tom Lee, as he sat knitting his brow and scowling his malevolent feelings at Dick Linton in the kitchen of the Angler's Inn. As the landlord had remarked to Mr Petty, the wind was keen and piercing, and rushed up the valley from the northwest so fast and furious, that all the cattle stood showing it their tails, and appeared as if they were impatiently looking out for the arrival of the cowherd to drive them to more snug quarters. The atmosphere was dry and clear and already the leaves had begun to drop from the trees, and whirled around in eddies as the wind went moaning round the corners of the woodlands, and the dust was driven before it along the solitary highway, blinding the weary traveller as he plodded on his way. In the kitchen of the village inn the fire burned brightly in the grate, and the large pewter plates in the old Delph case of polished oak reflected its flickering flame, giving an air of comfort to the apartment. Old Anthony's black favourite sheepdog stretched its limbs across the hearthstone in all the abandonment of true enjoyment. Anthony was attending to his outdoor duties, leaving his Dame the onerous task of keeping her quarrelsome customers from getting to the fighting point, to manage which she had to bring into play all the finesse of which she was capable; for, as they eyed one another across the hearth, every now and then the lighting of pent-up passion would dart from their fixed, burning eyeballs and would be followed by the muttering of distant thunder, and at such other times the storm would burst out threatening destruction to both the opposing parties, as well as to the good Dame for her well-meant officiousness. Then there would be a short lull till one of them had bethought himself of something that was sure to inflict another wound, and out would come the biting word or bitter taunt.

"Na, I'll not be browbeaten by thee Tom. Thou thinks that everybody should be frightened of thee; but I am not. I can show my face with thee anytime and anywhere. I tell thee what, if I'm poor, I'm honest, can thou say so?" And Dick Linton raised his voice to the highest pitch of passion, as he asked this question of Tom Lee who had been taunting him about his poverty.

"What does thou mean?" asked Tom with white quivering lips, a lowering brow charged with seven thunders, and fixed gaze which portended another storm.

"I mean what I say," doggedly answered Dick.

"What's that?" again asked Tom, with a fearful calmness, for considering what his opponent had said was an indirect accusation of being connected with the numerous burglaries committed in the neighbourhood, he was in a terrible rage, and the more so that it was the first accusation made in public.

"Why, who brack into John Jessop's house about a weeks sin' and stole three hams? That were ye. That's what they say."

"Who did?" impatiently asked Tom.

"I've seen a man this very day as says thou did", said Dick, at the same time measuring Tom's length with a dauntless eye; for he had risen as he had asked this last question.

"That man's a liar," shouted Tom as he made towards Dick, an' I'll mash every bone i' thy body."

"Why, what's to do now?" asked a deep sonorous voice, which was joined by the shrill tones of Dame Hodgson, who again interposed to preserve peace.

"Ye may well ask that, Mr Petty – the vagabonds, they've been like a dog and cat for the most of two hours, making an honest body's house as bad as th' Smuggler's Arms below yonder. I won't have it now, that's all about it. Sit ye down both of ye, or I'll fetch somebody that'll make you in quicksticks. I say sit down with ye."

"Yes, sit down and let me know what you are quarrelling about," requested Dr Petty, "you're always in hot water nowadays, Tom; How is that?"

"Who is it! I'll let that chap know who it is yet before I've done with him," growled Tom, as he unwillingly took his seat again, not half satisfied at being baffled in revenging himself, nor pleased at the doctor, who happened to come in at that juncture of affairs, for interfering with him. Besides he would rather have faced twenty Dick Lintons than the doctor just then; for he was apprehensive that so far from being a check upon Dick he would take pleasure in the proceedings, and seize the occasion to banter him a little himself in the same strain that Dick had been indulging in. Feeling in the doctor's power, Tom had quietly gulped his raillery, but in the present state he felt little disposed to do so.

"Why let me know now, then." Said Dick in answer to Tom's last observation; "only a bullying coward can threaten – only a cat can spring i' th' dark. Does thou think that thou can just do as thou likes, and everybody is to be so afraid of thee, so they dursn't speak to thee, same as if their mouth were sowed up. I told thee nought through what I could do, na crack that nut, will thou."

"I'll crack thy crown!" vociferated Tom, "if thou doesn't shut up!"

"Gently, Tom, gently," said the doctor, laughing at his vehemence, "what has Linton been saying to ruffle you so?"

"Said!" broke in Dick, "he's been as queer wi' me all th' day as if he'd slept in York Castle all th' last night, an' he'll get there yet, if he doesn't mind. I just give him a hint like about Jessop's hams, and there's all this to do. Touchiness isn't alas a sign o' innocence, mind; and I nobut told him what I heard, but I will say this, th' fellow told me he had a good guess who th' thief wor."

"Dick Linton", said Tom, rising again to his feet, burning with passion, "does thou mean to say if I stole Jessops hams, because if thou does I'll_____"

"Come, come, Tom, sit down and take things coolly, if ye did not steal them what's the use of going into such a rage about it; besides taking a ham or two is nothing to those other matters, you know, Tom, but we will keep them to ourselves; It's no use everybody knowing," continued he, winking at the same time as Dick; "and Dick over there shall not know a word about them, because he is so ready with his tongue, he cannot keep a secret."

Tom saw the wink and felt the sarcasm implied in the doctor's words. It was the first time that ever he had heard the doctor refer in public to what he knew of his doings, though he had often jibed him in private until it had produced a deep-seated feeling of uneasiness in his mind. That feeling there became intense, so much so, that the bad feeling he had just entertained towards Linton completely disappeared in the whirlpool of passion which the doctor had produced in his mind. He had not said much certainly, but enough to awaken from his slumbers a demon, who slumbered not again till he had goaded poor Tom onto the commission of a deed which cost him his life.

"I care little for what you know aboot me, Mr Petty. But supposing he did know summat, whatever Dick Linton is, you are a fine man to keep a secret," said Tom with assumed calmness and a deeper meaning which the doctor fully understood.

"Why I consider you have rather too hard on Dick. Ye carry yourself as if you were the most innocent man in the neighbourhood, and you know very well, Tom, that you are nothing of the sort, and as for keeping a secret, why that depends on yourself, Tom."

"Does it?" said Tom with an unnatural laugh, "then I'll see to it that it's kept."

"What do you mean?" asked the doctor, somewhat nettled.

"He's doing the same wi' you, doctor, as he's been doing wi' me," here broke in Dick, "he's just threatening your life, as I take it, that's all; but it'll hav' an end, it will."

"Ho, ho! A word of that sort, and I'll have him hung, the rascal! He knows that I can hang him at any time," said Petty, with considerable perturbation.

"Ye happen ye will not have a chance," said Tom, rising from his seat with a countenance livid with rage.

"I'm afraid Tom will get himself into trouble yet," said Petty.

"It'll be very well if he did get nob'dy else in," said Dick Linton, "I don't know about half them threats o' his, an' I'd advise ye to mind, doctor, that you don't give him th' chance to give you a sly knock; for, however he felt to'ards me, he seems to be fearful bitter to'ards ye, and as I take it, it's all because ye know rather more about him than he likes on."

"I believe he means ye no good," said Dame Hodgson, just then entering the room, "the ne'er-do-well, and to think that he should come here with his quarrelsome temper; but 'alls that well ends well', and be ye careful doctor. I don't just feel easy about him."

"Oh, he's only barking a bit, I've had him at it before; he daren't bite," said the doctor in a lightsome tone, in which he strove to hide an unaccountable fear that had come over him. Calling for his horse, he left the room and paced the grass-grown flags before the house in thoughtful mood. Soon old Anthony came round the corner leading his horse, which he was just in the act of mounting, when the good old Dame came to the door with an old-fashioned tumbler glass in her hand containing whiskey punch.

"Here, Mr Petty," said she, "the air is keen an' ye have a long ride before ye, just drink this, it'll warm th' cockles of your heart; an' as for Tom Lee, care nothing about him, only be careful, doctor, and keep out of his way, especially after nightfall."

"Oh, don't fear for me," said the doctor, as he took the glass from her, "a peaceful old age to ye both," continued he, bowing to Anthony and his wife. After draining the contents, he stooped down to return the glass, but a sudden movement of the horse caused it to drop to the ground. Instead of breaking, however, it rebounded from the pavement, when the dame caught it whole and sound.

"Lawks a me! Well, did ye ever see ought like that before, an' it's not broken." Said the astonished landlady.

We could not do that again," said the doctor, laughing," It's rather clever that."

"I doubt it's too clever; it bodes no good: there's something going to happen," exclaimed the dame, who seemed to be considerably perturbed with the singular phenomenon!

"Oh. Don't be alarmed," cried the doctor, as he rode off, "I've got the punch and I've got the glass all safe – never mind – all right – good-bye!" and the next moment he was out of sight.

"It may be all right." Said Anthony's spouse to him as he walked off to his work, shaking her head at the same time, "but I've my doubts and fears, I have – did ye ever know such a thing as a glass to fall that distance upon a hard pavement and not to break; it betokens ill luck to someone, it does."

"Oh, it happens to be so," quietly remarked Anthony, "an' I cannot see that we can mak' anything of it. Don't be so ready, wife, at meeting sorrow," and each took their several ways without a further remark.

CHAPTER III   THE RECONTRE

The shades of evening began gently to descend on mountain steep and verdant vale. The cloisters of the woodlands had finished their last anthem. The sheep on the lonely hillside had ceased their bleating. The cattle, tired of browsing, had sought out their favourite spot, and in cosy shelter, screened from the night wind, they had laid down to take their rest, and a deep silence reigned over the scene, only broken by the whispering breeze, 'the voice of the stream', as it sang along the solitary course, or the baying of some mastiff in the distant farmyard. As the shadows deepened, the various objects in the valley would have been hid from site, or woven into one opaque mass undistinguishable to the eye, had not the Crescent assisted by accompanying stars, scattered a few straggling rays of light which threw that dreamy repose o'er the land so congenial to romantic minds.

Over the of the hills and across the moorland wastes swept the moaning gale in fitful gusts, and the dim outline of the far-stretching mountains might be traced, irregularly cutting the horizon, for miles, while here and there jetted out into Wharfedale, a rocky promontory whose ruggedness was softened down with stunted oaks and firs, which, standing in bold relief against the northern sky, illuminated by the heavenly lights, appeared like Highland warriors rushing down upon some opposing foe, Kilnsey Crag rose out from the bosom of the veil like some giant spectre, who, chained to the spot, and doomed for thousands of years to gloomy solitude to expedite his guilt, yet reared his bold front against the starry sky as if defying the power which awarded him his destiny.

On the top of the Crag might have been seen a human figure, sometimes hurriedly walking along the edge of the precipice, at others, standing in a listening or musing attitude as if the individual were working himself up to the resolution of throwing himself down the yawning abyss and terminating an unhappy career of crime.

But such, reader, is not his intent. Who can he be, and what can be his object at such a time and place? See! A sudden gleam of light from the moon reveals the proportions and features of the one whom you have seen before, though he has endeavoured partially to disguise himself. Need you be told that that tall figure, that brawny arm, that lowering brow, that compressed lip, and that fiery eye belonged to Tom Lee - his breast is a volcano of passion; and fuel has been thrown into it during the day which makes the fire of vengeance so burn within, that until he has carried out the desperate design which he has formed, it cannot be appeased. The words of Dr Petty have sunk deep into his heart, and while the doctor lives he does not feel safe, and he is now contemplating the commission of an act which will not only add to his other crimes, but will overtop them all in the fearful guilt it will involve.

Like the moth which flutters around the flame, narrowing the circle till it perish, or the bird arrested by the fatal glare of the basilick, and not able to get beyond its attractive influence till it fall a prey to the destroyer, so Tom Lee has got entangled in the strong meshes which the tempter within has thrown securely around him, and one idea only took possession of his mind, the demon wrote it in characters of fire on his brain - Petty must die. Ever since he had left the Angler's Inn, the afternoon had been spent in concocting means for the accomplishment of his object, and having ascertained that the doctor had gone up the Dales on one of his accustomed rounds, and did not expect to be back till late that night, he determined to carry out his intentions upon him as he returned, thinking the opportunity of favourable one. The place where he now stood, nursing his foul design, commanded the highway for a considerable distance above, and he was there for the purpose of listening for the sound of the horse's feet announcing the doctor's approach when he intended to cross the valley by a shortcut, and waylay him at a lonely spot on the opposite side of the valley. He had not to wait long before he heard the trampling sound of the nag's hooves as it came along the road at a brisk trot; When he immediately took the direction leading away to

Geastrills or Ghostrills, a lonely and wooded place by the river, some distance below.

Knowing that the doctor would call at Anthony Hodgkin's, and stop a little while, he did not hurry, but went leisurely along, brooding over the work before him with those revengeful feelings which nerve men to the Commission of deeds of darkness. The Geastrills was a spot seldom visited by the inhabitants of the district of; and by the superstitious portion of them it was regarded as a haunted place. It was so sequestered, and nature was in such a wild state, that, arrived among its intricacies, wandering among its gloomy shades, and listening to the hoarse voice of the river as its waters rolled heavily along between its banks, covered with rank wild-grass, flags, ferns, and the fantastic roots of trees laid bare in some places by the rushing floods it only required a slight stretch of the imagination to believe one's self transported into the backwards of America.

In some places among the rocks the waters were of great depth there were numerous eddies, and the suction was so great that he was daring indeed who committed himself to their treacherous bosom. In doing so several had drawn into the hollow caverns beneath and lost their lives. Some imagine that they ghosts wandered about the scene of their death, and at different times their death shrieks were to be heard resounding far and wide, filling the heart of the related traveller with the most anxious fears, and causing him to quicken his steps from the vicinity of a place so lonely, gloomy, and forbidding.

It was in this place Tom Lee resorted as being a spot most congenial with his present state of mind, and here he intended to remain till the moment came for the dark deed to be done, of which he was now meditating the accomplishment. When that moment came he had only to thread his way from the river side up to the Grassington road, a short distance above, and unexpectedly fall upon the doctor, - but Tom Lee, blinded with passion as he was, did not think of the final issues of the deed he was meditating during that night; The devil within him so effectively drew the film over his visual organ, that he dared not to penetrate the future, but yielded himself up to the influence of the predominant passion which now governed him.

The doctor reached the Angler's Inn very much fatigued with his long ride, but the cup of good tea which the Hostess prepared for him proved very refreshing, and the agreeable chat which they had over it was no less enjoyed by him; indeed, he felt so cosy and comfortable as time slipped away without his being aware of the advanced hour of the night; but the grey-faced clock, which, in oaken case occupied the same position it had done for a century of years in the corner of the kitchen, striking the hour of eleven, reminding him that he had some four miles before him, and he at once requested that his horse might be brought around from the stable. While old Anthony was fetching his horse, and he was putting on his overcoat, the dame made him a glass of negus, and bringing it to him, said,

"You shall not drink this inside the house, doctor, and mind and not let the glass fall again as you did this afternoon - it's the same glass, and perhaps will break if you let it fall a second time. My goodness me! But was it not a singular thing, doctor? I cannot get it off my mind but there's something going to happen, wrong."

"Oh, you women are privileged beings, you are always allowed to imagine things a little your own way, you know; and should you make something out of nothing, my gallantry forbids us laughing at you but in this case I am indeed tempted to smile at the seriousness with which you invest such a trivial and accidental circumstance as that of a glass falling without breaking. If we had time, most likely we would make out a reason by which to account for it, but here's my horse, and I must go. Good night."

"Good night, doctor; but privileged or not privileged to indulge our bits of whims, as some of you are pleased to call them, I only hope not in this case my presentiment may only not be realised in any harm happening to you."

"Thank you; I hope the same. But we will talk these matters over next time I see you. Tom Lee has already gone too far in crime to do anything of the sort you apprehend, but as i said before, his bark is louder than his bite is dangerous," and the doctor started on his way to Grassington.

"My kind regards to Mrs Petty," cried Dame Hodgson as his form disappeared in going down the hillside leading to Coniston-bridge.

The night was cold but fine. The sparkling vault of heaven was a magnificent sight to behold. Not a single cloud obscured its glory, and the innumerable stars were so intensely bright that, in the twinkling, golden beams they emitted, they appeared instinct with life - beautiful did they look in the deep setting of blue. Perhaps nothing gives man a profound idea of the vastness of boundlessness of immensity that when he gazes on the face of the heavens on such a night - nothing more expands his mind, and makes him feel his own insignificance more deeply; and how, at such a time, is the searching, enquiring spirit led to reflect upon future life – 'the land beyond the flood.' Dr Petty was a man of keen observation and to him. He had a well-developed intellect, a large sympathetic heart which lovingly embraced both nature and man. His perceptive and reflective faculties were in a constant exercise, whatever the scene nature presented to him, or diversified the character of those with whom he from time to time came in contact. Firmly established in good moral principles, which his general conduct fully proved, but, being conscious that his motives were right and his intentions good, he laboured precious little to convince those about him of the fact, and he was constantly outdone, therefore, by the namby-pamby jabberings of professionals, I did not consequently stand as high as these in the opinion of those self-constituted judges of human conduct who are to be found in every little community, and who imagine that from the prominent position they occupy in it, wisdom dwells with them alone. He had his failings who has not? But he deserved a better fate than that which awaited him. Engaging on that night scene, he was more than ordinarily impressed with its grandeur, but he did not feel as elated with the purifying and ennobling thoughts which it suggested as he usually did; on the contrary, he felt a sadness of heart which he could not account for, a feeling which is expressed in the utterance of the word 'farewell.'

He felt as if gazing for the last time on scenes both familiar and dear to him; And strange to say, if he darted a thought to the home scene, it appeared dim and indistinct - he could not fully realise it - he felt as if cut off from his family, and was not destined again to join it. Under the uneasiness which this thought produced in his mind, he put spurs to his horse, anxious to reach home in defiance of some dark impending fate which seemed to hang over him. The rattling of his horse's hooves might have been heard as he sped over the bridge, breaking the silence which reigned around, and the Wharfe caught in the shadow of both rider and horse in passing.

On he went, last in a most perplexing reverie; as he neared Grass Wood, however, the horse rather shied and slackened it space. Thinking that the shadows of the wood had brought up his steed, he thought he would let it take its own time through the wood, but the beast had seen what he in his abstractions had failed to do. The gate was closed, and protruding beyond the moss-grown wall which enclosed the wood was the head of a human being, with fixed fiery eyes, that expressed a foul design on the part of their processor. Unconscious of such close proximity of anyone, the doctor proceeded to open the gate which he had now reached. Having got through, he bent down to fasten it again, and while doing so he heard a rustling noise, but before he could raise himself to look in the direction whence it proceeded, a heavy blow from a bludgeon brought him reeling from the saddle to the ground. The startled and now riderless horse galloped away towards Grassington, leaving its prostrate master in deadly struggle with his murderous assailant. Though the blow stunned him, it did not deprive him of all consciousness.

"Murderous villain!" shouted he when he saw who the person was who had attacked him, and while warding off a second blow intended for his head, "I'll live yet," and he wrenched the weapon from Tom Lee, for it was he, as the reader no doubt will have some surmised.

"Aye, but not for long!" hissed between the lips of his assailant, "ye know too much for me," and falling upon the doctor again, a fierce struggle ensued. On grappling with each other, they fell to the ground, the doctor uppermost; for nerved by the feelings of the most violent rage at the baseness of Lee's design he grasped him with superhuman strength. The struggle lasted for some time and Tom was likely to be worsted, but succeeded at length in drawing a clasp-knife from his pockets, he plunged it into the doctor's side, when, with a wild shriek, which awakened the murderer to a horror of his guilt, the murdered man released his hold and rolled on his back apparently lifeless. To make sure his work was done he plunged the fatal blade once more into the already motionless body, and then dragged it under the shadow of the wall.

And there Tom Lee stood in the dim moonlight, the murderer of Dr Petty. He had accomplished his object. He would now feel satisfied. He had let them see who was the most cunning, and strong, and devilish. They must not think of being too many for him; and now that Petty was 'done for', as he called it, he could be easy as the demon revenge, who had ruled on the throne of his heart all day, controlled every feeling, had constantly whispered to him would be the case after the perpetration of the deed; and now that same demon vacated that throne with such a horrible and unearthly laugh at the gullibility of his victim, that Tom Lee shook from head to foot like an aspen leaf, and another demon - the demon remorse - reigned in his stead.

And oh! The sulphurous, suffocating darkness of that reign - the iron rule, the crushing tyranny of that savage despot! He was so bewildered and frustrated for the moment with what he had done, that he did not know what next to do. Remorse so lacerated him with his torturing whip (whose every thong was a scorpion which tore his very vitals at every blow) that he writhed in the deepest agony. The heaven on the earth seemed ready to cry out 'there is blood on my soul.' It rang in his ears.

Yet something must be done. The body must be removed, and all traces of the dark deed must be obliterated; and steps must be taken at once, lest the morning light should reveal the terrible secret, or some passer-by should see evidence of the monstrous act. Covering the body of the doctor as well as he could with rank grass and weeds which grew in profusion in the wood, he set off for Grassington hardly knowing what to do. Fear gave swiftness to his heels, and he soon reached the village. Nearly all its inhabitants had retired to rest, only here and there was to be seen a light streaming from the chamber-lattice of the cottages as the inmates were preparing to commit themselves to their peaceful slumbers; and Tom Lee, the burglar, and now murderer, would have given the wealth of nations to be in possession of their innocence and easy consciences. He glided up the village St as noiselessly and as stealthily as he could. On reaching its own house all was silent and in darkness; and though an inn, all the company had departed. He gave a gentle tap at the kitchen window, when his wife, who had been sitting by the dying embers in the kitchen great, and uneasy at his prolonged absence, and momentarily expecting his return, immediately unlocked the door, and eagerly questioned him about the cause of his absence. He at once told her what had taken place, making her acquainted with every particular. At first she was horrified at the recital, but being aware of his former proceedings, and to a great extent an abettor therein, she feared more for the consequences that might follow his night's work then she felt compunction for the guilt which had been contracted.

Various were the plans they discussed for the effectual hiding of the body, and in their perturbed state forgot the possibility of being overheard. At last she bethought herself that probably Jack Sharp, the apprentice, who slept in the room above and who had only retired to bed a short time before, might have heard the tale.

This was a fresh source of fear to them both, but they soon determined to know whether he had or not, by Tom's going up into the bedroom and ascertaining whether he was asleep or not. If he found the young man had overheard anything, he had made-up his mind what to do in the matter. Accordingly he crept softly into the sleeping apartment of Jack Sharp. Jack had overheard the whole conversation, and was completely paralysed with fear; but when he heard Tom ascending the stairs he trembled from head to foot. What was he to do? Feign sleep? There was no time for further reflection; summoning all his nerve, he stretched himself on his side, and put on the appearance of deep sleep. Tom approached the bed with a candle in one hand and a knife in the other, and narrowly scanned Jack's face for a considerable time. Jack's heart beat violently, and the pain he endured in forcing himself to keep in one position in such a state of mind was so great that he could not command his countenance till Tom had completed his scrutiny. He opened his eyes, and on seeing the weapon in Tom's hand, he sprung from the bed horrified.

"So thou heard, has thou?" said Tom, sternly eyeing him.

Jack had not the power to answer, being thrilled with terror at the thought that Tom intended to take his life, "I've, I've," at length he stammered out, but could not proceed.

"Thou'st overheard us, has thou?" again asked Tom, at the same time approaching him.

"I, I – I've nobbut heard part – yer-e-er n-n-not going to take my life, are ye?" asked Jack.

"On two conditions I am not," said Tom approaching Jack still nearer.

"What-a-t are they?" eagerly enquired Jack, in great fear of bodily harm.

"As to what thou's heard, be it more or less, promise this minute that 'mum's' the word – that thou willn't tell any living soul. Swear it!"

"I'se tell nobody, I'se sure – I little dare," said Jack, anxious to save his life, "an' I'll swear ought ye want me to."

"Well, thou knows me," said Tom, brandishing the knife he held in his hand, "an' I'm fit to think that thou little dare tell a word – if thou does, thou knows what follows. Don thy clothes and go wi' me."

Jack felt a little relieved, and proceeded forthwith to dress himself, but while doing so, wondered very much where Tom wanted him to go, and what he wanted him to do. He hastened, however, to join his master, who had already descended the stairs, and who, with a sack thrown over his arms, was preparing to leave the house. Tom having made his wife acquainted with his intentions, they set out into the shades of the night. The somewhat heavy gales which a few hours before had swept across the bleak moorlands, and among the moaning woods, had subsided, and the heavy masses of cloud which for the last hour had been gathering, became now almost stationary, nearly obscuring the face of the heavens. Now and then a glimpse of the moon or a cluster of stars could be caught through the cloud fissures, but these soon closed up and a patch of landscape momentarily lighted up, and was again left in shadow. That solemn stillness reigned over the valley so suggestive of profound thought, but all these things were unperceived by Jack Sharp and his master as they quietly hurried through the village, the latter being intent on the prosecution of his plans, in the accomplishing of which expedition, seemed to be of the utmost important, and the former wondering what the object of their sudden journey could be.

On they sped; and it was only when they entered Grass Wood that Tom divulged his intentions to his apprentice. His purpose was to remove the body of the murdered man to a place of security. Various plans have been thought of by him in his bewildered state of mind, but at last he had come to the determination of secreting the doctor's remains in the recesses of a deep rocky glen little above the spot where the fatal struggle had taken place. It was not without fear that Tom, hard and as he was, approached the scene of the murder; But time was not to be frittered away, and the fear of detection allowed of no hesitancy - it must be done. He went to the place where he had deposited the body, but was horror-stricken to find it was not there. Had he been watched? Had the doing of the deed been witnessed by someone else who had removed the body in his absence? Was the dreadful secret out? Awful was the torture he endured for a few moments, but hearing a deep groan at a little distance from him he went in the direction whence the same preceded, and found the object of his search. It appeared life was not extinct when Tom left his victim. Soon after his departure for the village he had had a short slight interval of consciousness, and, though nearly dead from loss of blood, feeling that life was fast oozing from him, he managed to crawl a few yards towards the pathway in the hope of attracting the attention of some passer-by. Tom finding that his victim was not yet dead, suddenly bethought him not the best way of binding Jack Sharp to secrecy was to make him finish the dreadful work. This Jack, who greatly feared that his own life might be sacrificed did he object, was not long in doing. Searching in an adjoining hedge he soon found a stake with which he wants proceeded to perform the horrible task assigned him. Of course the prostrated doctor could offer no resistance, and the work was soon done.

Excepting the sounds of the night-winds as they gently whispered among the leaves of the trees, or the sound of the Wharfe as he took his solitary course down the vale, nothing but the dull heavy death-blows disturbed the reigning silent; And strangely those sounds fell upon his ear, wakening Echo - the spirit of the surrounding hills - who from her dark recesses beheld the commission of the dreadful deed, and then, rising among the stars, conveyed the intelligence to the great spirit of the universe.

As soon as the doctor was dead, they lost no time in getting the body into the sack which Tom had brought for the purpose of comparing it to a place of secrecy. Tom raised the strange burden onto Jack's back, and they forthwith commenced their toilsome ascent towards a deep rocky glen which opened into the heart of the mountain at a little distance above the scene of the murder. On they toiled, anxious to bury their guilt in the bowels of the earth, till at last they reached the opening leading into the glen, who sides rose almost perpendicularly to a great height, covered in some places with thick brushwood, and in others, massive fragments of rock overhung the glen with frowning aspect, as it threatened to rush down on those who dared to enter into its gloomy precincts. Just as they had passed through the opening and were passing into the shadow, a spectral with one hand raised towards the starlit heavens and the other stretched towards them, clenched, and violently shaken at them as if given expression to the feeling of vengeance which lighted up every lineament of its ghastly countenance dashed across the glen in gigantic proportions, and disappeared into the distance. On seeing the dreadful apparition, or thinking he saw one (for it was neither more nor less than moonbeams momentarily darting through a cloud fissure and falling in fantastic shapes on the dark background of the glen - taking in the excited state of his mind and form of the phantom) Jack Sharp threw down the body of the doctor and was making off as fast as he could, when Tom seized him and again threatened his life if he refused, compelled him to remain and assist in hiding the doctor's remains. Long they searched for a suitable place, and when they found one, longer did they labour to effectively secrete the sack and its content, and extremely careful were they not to leave the least trace of their night's work.

And did they succeed? Such a secret is safe nowhere in God's universe. Nature, with its outraged laws, thunders forth its own anathemas, against the guilty culprit, and no man's conscience is stout and strong enough to bear in peace and quiet the terrible burden which murder imposes upon it. The perpetrator of such a deed might prevent detection for a time, but eventually, by some means or other, murder will out.

When Tom and his apprentice had finished their work to the satisfaction of the former, warned by the approach of the grey-clad pilgrim, twilight, who was making his way over the eastern hills the advance-courier of the great king of day, they directed their steps by the most unfrequented paths to the village of Grassington.

CHAPTER IV   GUILT SUSPECTED BUT NOT DETECTED

On the morning following the events recorded in our last chapter there was no small stir in the usually quiet village of Grassington. It was no unusual thing for Dr Petty to be absent from home the whole night long, as he was frequently engaged in urgent cases and quite unexpectedly, detained on his way, to attend to the duty of his profession. So often was this the case, that his family felt no uneasiness at his absence, and would retire to rest at their accustomed hour, all but old Robert, the doctor's servant, whose duty was it, being altogether uncertain at what hour his master would return. to stop up some time after the family had retired to rest, to be in readiness to attend to the horse, and, being proud of the animal, he often stayed up till a very late hour to attend to it himself, as the doctor's idea of the amount of care necessary to be bestowed upon four-footed beasts did not at all suit old Roberts notions on that subject.

But when we read with waiting in vain hour after hour for his master, even the strong affection for old Dobbin did give way to his need for rest, and he would march off to bed giving utterance to his firm opinion "that his master cared far more for his patients than for his horse." Honest old Robert thought on the morning in question that when the night before he uttered this speech, his kind master lay a corpse in the neighbouring word. Rising early he preceded to this table to see whether Dobbin had returned; Or, if not, to prepare for his arrival. Great was his surprise when, on reaching the back part of the premises, he saw the doctor's horse standing close to the stable door, pawing the ground as if impatient of standing at the wrong side of the said door. He looked about for his master, Thinking he had only just dismounted, but no master was to be seen. He was puzzled to make out why Dobbin was thus left. He called out, but no one answered. "Well, this is a case, how's ever," said he to himself, "he's never played a trick of this sort before. I'se often said he's no feelings for a horse, but this caps Dolly - it does! To think he must leave it standing here after this guide. There's summat wrong, I'm sure there is."

At this moment Dobbin neighed and pawed the ground impatiently to get in. "Hear ye there," said Robert, "it fair talks like a Christian, it does" and patting Dobbins neck, he led it into the stable, and preceded at once to attend its requirements, not however, without frequently pausing to wonder what could be the cause of the horse being left standing in the yard in that manner, "there's summat wrong," said he after he had made Dobbin alright, "an' I'se bound to know what it is, too," and he made to the doctor's dwellings to make enquiry.

"Is the master in?" asked he of the servant girl whom he found lighting the fire in the kitchen.

"I don't ken, I'se sure, Robert," announced the girl, looking out from her night cap, and whose rosy cheeks and bright, twinkling eyes told of a good night's rest.

"Then ye should ken," returned Robert rather snappishly for he began to feel very uneasy about his master.

"Deary me!" Said the girl, surprised at the old man's manner, so unusual for him, "I ken which side o'er th' bed ye've gotten out of this morning."

"Go this minute an' inquire oh th' missus, and dunna ye stand there gaping at me."

"What's come over ye this morning?" asked the astonished girl.

"Has master come home, I want to know? Go an' ask his missus, will thou?" shouted old Robert.

"What is there to do?" enquired Mrs Petty, just then entering the kitchen; for when the doctor did not return home she always rose early.

"I wanted to know if the master had come home," said Robert, "but that lass wouldn't stir a peg, continued he, looking vinegar at the girl.

"He has not," said the doctor's wife. "Why are you so anxious?"

"Why if he hasn't there's summat wrong, that's all."

"What do you mean?" asked the good lady, beginning to feel alarmed at the man's appearance and manner.

"I mean that when I went out into th' yard, I found Dobbin standing at the stable door wi' a hide wet as Gideon's fleece, and thought — there's summat wrong."

"Oh dear, Robert, you make me tremble! What can there be wrong? The doctor stayed away all night many a time before now."

"Yes, he has, missus," said Robert, beginning to feel alarmed himself, as well as fidgety, "he has for sure. But you know he's always come'd back with Dobbin afore this time. But I'm tired o' standing here – I'll go an' try if I can hear ought on him, he may be up I' th' toon somewhere." Continued he, making at the same time towards the door.

"Go, Robert," said Mrs Petty, "bring me news as soon as you can - and –." But the old man was gone, and what the remaining "and" of her unfinished sentence prefaced she had not the opportunity of telling.

"Oh, Nelly!" said Mrs Petty, continuing, partly addressing the girl, and partly soliloquizing, at the same time seating herself in the corner chair by the ingle side, "I begin to fear Roberts words may be true – what a fearful dream it was - he looked so lovingly, so beseechingly at me, and I could not help him - and then, that parting look. Oh, how sad my heart felt! How sad it feels now! Nelly, there's something wrong! It's something unusual after all, for Dobbin to come home by himself. I fear it augurs no good," and then she became abstracted, and seemingly lost in anxious contemplation.

Meanwhile old Robert proceeded on his mission to gather some intelligence of his missing master. Twilight began to creep into the shadowy corners and narrow lanes in and surrounding the village of Grassington. A few of the early risers of the village had issued from their peaceful homes to attend to their several occupations, some to their husbandry, and some were setting out to the lead mines. Robert took up the town-gate, and inquired of everyone he met with if They had seen anything of the doctor; but he could get no information. Passing up the thoroughfare of the village he at length came to the blacksmith's shop where the hammer was being busily plied and the sound of the anvil echoed through every part of the village. The fire was white with heat, and the burning sparks flew in all directions under the vigorous blows of Tom Lee and his apprentice, Jack

Sharp, who were busy sharpening the tools belonging to some miners who were impatiently waiting for the same. Old Robert, knowing that the doctor occasionally dropped in to have a little chat with Tom, thought that he might have done so then, or, if not, Tom might possibly have seen him, or be able to give some information respecting him. He therefore called in to ask Tom if he had seen him.

"Seen th' doctor, Tom?" asked Bobby.

"I've been o'er thrang this morning for ought but getting these things ready for Jim Brown here, an' he's grumbling like a bear wi' sore teeth because they woren't done last night. Odds fish, man! A body nobbut can do what he can," and Tom worked away with the air of one who had not a moment's time to give a thought to anything but his own business.

"That's reight enough," returned Robert, but I thought doctor might a popped in to crack a joke wi' thee. He must be somewhere in the' town. If he isn't, there's summat wrong, that's all."

"How's summat wrong?" asked Jim Brown. "What does thou mean, Bobby?"

"I means I found Dobbin standing at th' stable-door this morning, but I cannot find th' doctor."

"Bigow! But that's rather queer, isn't it, Tom?" asked Jim, as he gathered up the tools which the smith had just finished.

"It's queer enough," briefly responded Tom, whose pale face and sweat-beaded brow, mistaken by the bystanders for exhaustion consequent upon his morning's hard labour, told plainly his mind.

"Bigow, Bobby," said Brown, as, followed by his companions, he started off for the mines, "I'd hunt th' doctor up or I'd mak sumb'day hear me. There's summat I do not like about it. Doesn't thou say that reins were broken, an' all miry, as if th' horse had stepped on to 'em an' dragged 'em through th' mire."

"Yes, they were," Robert affirmed.

"Then dunnat loose a minute in finding th' doctor's whereabouts. It looks very queer, it does," saying which, Jim Brown and his companions left the smithy with an all-engrossing topic for the day.

"Then ye haven't seen him at all this morning, Tom?" asked Robert, preparing to leave the shop.

"I tell ye, Bobby, he not been here this morning, that I've seen, with which reply old Robert set out in search of the missing man, persisting in the conviction that there was something wrong.

In a very short time it was known throughout the village doctor petty could not be found, together with the fact that his horse had returned riderless, with broken reins, bespattered with Mire. Every bit of fresh news in sequestered hamlets is laid hold of by the inhabitants with avidity, and soon becomes the common property of the little community. Before sundown everyone was speaking to everyone in Grassington about the mysterious disappearance of its medical man. Through the day little knots of persons might have been seen eagerly discussing the probable causes of it; and everyone tested his or her ingenuity to the utmost in trying to give a satisfactory explanation of the affair accompanied with all kinds of gestures, winks, nods, and pointing of the fore-finger, shaking of heads, pulling long faces, and throwing out the most convincing innuendos, teamed with meaning, relative to the foregones in the doctor's life and his present circumstances. Some thought he and his could not agree; Others asserted that his debts pressed heavily upon him, and he had run away from the impending crash. One went so far as to say that TI once heard the doctor talk about America, and how people got on there.

But the news did not stop there - Grassington it flew in all directions. Scouring parties went out in search of him; for his distracted wife, who had begun to think that some serious accident had befallen him, could not rest until every means had been tried to ascertain his whereabouts and the cause of his absence. One of these parties took the road to Kilnsey and separated from one another so as to sweep the country in that direction, yet they kept within hailing distance. On they went through Grass Wood, one of them going along the regular pathway. On reaching the end of the word farthest from Grassington, his attention was attracted to the place which seemed to have been more than commonly trodden, and that only very recently. He at once called his comrades to the spot, and they all came to the conclusion that there was every indication of a struggle having taken place. The deep indentations made in the ground by shoe-heels, the broken-down underwood all around the spot, and the disturbed appearance of the gravel on the pathway, as if someone had been laid or rolled upon it, helped them to certain conclusions which lead again to the long faces, winks, nods, and hints of something very calamitous.

And when they came to one spot and found the gravel of a reddish cast, or, at least, thought it was, for it was getting dark, and they could scarcely discern colour very accurately, they were more than ever of the opinion that there had been foul work, for they set it down that what had dyed the sand was blood. With grave faces and important strides, they posted on towards Kilnsey, to gain, if possible, more information respecting the doctor, feeling that what they might hear would only tend to prove what they suspected, and for the sake of the doctor's family, very much feared to know.

They soon reached Kilnsey, and went at once to the Angler's Inn, as the place most likely to afford the information they wanted.

Jerry Fenton, the self-elected leader of the party - a person who delighted to be meddling with other people's concerns, who for talking was a veritable magpie, and who on this occasion was of very great self-importance - walked into the Inn, and found three or four persons in the kitchen listening to the somewhat vehement remarks of one who appeared to be rather the worst for the quantity of Dame Hodgson's 'best' he had imbibed. Jerry recognised the man at once.

"Dick, lad, how is thou?" enquired he of this person.

"I'se all reight, in one sense, but not in another," replied Dick.

"Thoo'rt talking with humour, howsomever," remarked Jerry, "bud in what sense art thou wrong?"

"Why, it's just here, see this," answered Dick, eyeing at the same time the companions of Jerry, sometimes I drink ale because i like it but I'm drinking today because one of your Grassington folk nettled me, yesterday in this very room."

"Who do you mean? asked Jerry.

"Who do I mean?" shouted Dick. Clenching his fists and beating the air, I mean that dewn-looking rascal, our Tom Lee. "What does thou mean, Jerry? He was up here yesterday, bullying and driving all before him, just as he's in the habit o' doing, thou knows, an' because I snapped him a bit, by th' heart, he threatened my life?"

"Oh, aye!" said Jerry.

"Yes, an' that weren't all! He threatened our Grassington doctor, too. At least, I took it so!"

"Did he, mistress?" asked Dick, turning to Dame Hodgson who, at that moment had entered the room.

"Oh, bud I would like to have my fling at him, I could so," continued dick, before anybody else could speak.

"Now, now, Dick Linton," said the landlady, "ye should not give way to your feelings in that way, you know what Tom is, you shouldn't take any notice of him," and she proceeded to relate what had taken place the day before to the newcomers.

They looked at one another with elongated faces, and after sundry winks, nods, and shaking of heads, Jerry, their mouthpiece, dealt out all the news from Grassington.

"Now then, mistress do I speak too strong new?" broke in Dick Linton. "I'll bet my head to a penny piece, that Tom Lee has murdered__"

"Hold, hold, Dick!" cried several voices at once. "be careful what ye say."

"Well anyone, ye cannot stop me from thinking it. But it'll come to it yet - he will, an' he deserves it he does."

The whole present checked Dick in the rash expressions to which he was about to give utterance, yet, after both parties had compared notes, they felt as strongly convinced that Tom Lee was in some way connected with the mysterious affair, as they felt backwards to say so, in as many words. One consideration why they did not venture to tell their thoughts freely was, though the doctor was missing, and though there were many convincing proofs to their mind that he had been foully dealt with - such as Tom Lee's threatenings, the return of the horse without its master, together with what they had seen in Grass Wood - yet, notwithstanding all this, how did they know what he would turn up. They thought it prudent, therefore to restrain their tongues, or, if they did state their opinions, they did so confidentially. And, in the shape of a running secret, in a very short time the whole district was well informed of all particulars, and almost everyone identified Tom Lee as the principal actor in the mysterious affair.

The party returned the same night to Grassington, and related what they had heard to hundreds of eager listeners. What they had to relate only served to confirm the worst fears of the doctor's wife. The spark of hope she had permitted herself to indulge in was quenched, and with her there was a fearful look of trial and misery. She was completely prostrated some might suspect, but her heart whispered she would see her husband no more, and under the pressure of the forebodings she became seriously ill, and remained so for some weeks. But how fared it was Tom Lee, and what was he doing?

The night was dark and lowering. The wind rushed down the valley with one continuous sweep, and loudly whistled over the tops of the pine-clad trees, there was every appearance of the approach of a storm. The hour was just only eleven as two persons, disguised, might have been seen stealthily creeping out of the upper end of Grassington. One, a young-looking person, led by the bridle a grey pony, and seemed anxious to keep the animal on one side of the stone covered road to prevent any noise being made, while the other keenly peered out from between the drooping brim of a slouched hat and the heavy folds of a dark muffler, to see if their movements were observed by anyone. After having got some distance from the village, and got onto an unfrequented road leading up to the moorlands, they seemed to be rather more at their ease, though they did not abate their speed in the least, apparently being on some business which required both expedition and secrecy. What the nature of the business was, however, there was nothing about them to indicate, accept what appeared to be a spade, which the elder of the two carried on his shoulder, and whose outline could be caught between the observer and the cloud driven sky, as he who carried it walked along the mountain-ridge. On they went in silence. Now and then the young man would address a word or two to his companion, but got no answer. The slouched hat went on his way lost in his own deep cogitations. The driving wind beat against his breast, accompanied with large cold ice-drops; but he was impervious to the raging elements of the heavy storm that was settling in. A far fiercer storm waged within that breast - compared with which the outside storm was a calm summer's day.

So far from heeding the pitiless, pelting storm through which he dragged his stalwart form, he felt it to be congenial to the frame of mind that he was in. The rushing wind was music, and the darkness which hid him was just what he desired. It was Tom Lee, and he had done a deed which fearless as he was, shook his soul to its very foundations. Only the night before he thought he had removed the doctor's remains to a place of security, and left no traces to the spot; but the anxious enquiries made after the doctor, the searching parties who, during the day, had gone forth to discover his whereabouts, and the general commotion of the village, had made the day one of agony to him.

To say that there was no remorse felt by him for the deed had done would not be saying the truth. The fiend remorse, to some extent, lacerated him; but the fiend whose crushing foot was grinding him to dust, was fear. After all the precaution he had taken, was it not possible that some of the parties that had been out during the day searching for the missing doctor, might meet with something that would put them on the scent of the mortal remains hid in the rocky Glen? While the doctor lived he had imagined his own well-being was insecure. This was the thought which had goaded him on to the commission of the dark deed which had branded his forehead, but now he felt more insecure than ever, and the loud laugh -heard above the storm that was raging round him - of the phantom of remorse, who only the day before had abdicated the throne of his heart, and who, in his disordered imagination, he saw careering on the driving blasts, filled his soul with mortal terror. Such were some of the thoughts as he hurried on his dark some way.

After proceeding for some time, they at length approached the top of a somewhat deep glen.

"What are we to do wi' the galloway, Tom, while we're down in th' gully?" asked Jack Sharp, for it was he who accompanied Tom Lee on this expedition.

"We mustn't fasten it to a tree, ye oaf -who'd say that but thee?" gruffly answered Tom, with a mind ill at ease; "and be wary what thou'rt doing, or maybe thou will have to follow the doctor," continued he, by way of nerving Jack to the deed before him.

Nearing the Glen, they led to the pony under the deep shadow of some trees, untied it to the bole of one of them, and soon descended into the gloomy depths of the Glen. Down they went, until having arrived at the rocky precipitous part of the same, they preceded to clear away the brushwood which curtained the opening of a cave under the rocks. This they did as noiselessly as possible, for Tom was racked with the fear of attracting the attention of either poacher or keeper who might be in the vicinity. They disappeared for a short time in the cave, but soon issued forth again bearing the terrible burden of poor Petty's remains. Jack assisted Tom in getting the sack onto his back, and they slowly and cautiously began their ascent up the glen. This, owing to the unevenness of the path, was no slight work, for now they would be up to their knees in water, and then they would stumble over the pieces of rock and slippery stones that were scattered in their way. They carried the dead by turns, and they had nearly reached the top of the glen when they were startled by a strange noise which preceded from an aged oak which grew its long bare branches across the glen directly above their heads. Jack was carrying the sack, but on hearing the noise, his strength completely forsook him. His legs refused to do their duty and the burden rolled off his back.

With his hair like the rump of a cat, and confronting and fierce dog, he stammered out -

"What's that, Tom? Is it doctor's spirit or the old chap that's coming to fetch us?"

For a moment Tom stood motionless as a post, it could not have answered Jack for all the wealth of Wharfedale, so paralysed was he in fear. His strained eyes were fixed in the direction whence the sound preceded, and the sweat oozed out of every pore of his body. The strong, the daring Tom Lee stood trembling like an aspen leaf in the middle of the glen terrified by the creaking of a large withered bough which dangled from the trunk of the tree under which he was passing, swaying to and fro by the wind, and his terror was complete when a large black raven darted out of the same tree, flapping its wings and uttering wild screams, as it swept down the glen, scared by the living and the dead. Oh, the terrible power of a guilty conscience!

After the bird had flown away, and Tom had ascertained the cause of the creaking sound which had arrested their progress up the glen (which by going up to the trunk of the tree he was enabled to do so) He rejoined Jack, and found him still on his knees scarcely reassured, though there was no other sign of the presence of the 'Old Chap', while Tom had been sweating through fear, the same feeling had almost frozen Jack into an ice-lump. Time was passing, however, and they began to see the necessity for action; they therefore shouldered their burden again, and preceded on their way, and were not long in reaching the top of the glen. Securing the load to the back of the grey pony, they took the direction of the pasture lands, skirting the vast moorlands a few miles above. Though Tom had somewhat recovered from his fright, the demon fear kept fast hold of his heartstrings, and on he went as fast as the pony could ascend the hill with its burden, thinking to find a little more ease after he had carried out his present design.

The road they pursued led past one or two solid tree farmhouses on the hills, and, on nearing the last of these, they were somewhat started to observe a light streaming through one of the casements. What were they to do? A single ray of light, even from a midnight lamp, or the sound of a single sere, whirling leaf, was quite sufficient, in their circumstances, to fill them with the greatest apprehensions and dread. After consulting a little while they agreed that Jack should proceed first and reconnoitre the premises, and getting quietly to the door, should hold it fast, less the noise of the pony's feet at that untimely hour, attracting the attention of any of the inmates who might be up, should bring them to the door to see who might be passing. Jack did so; but Tom leading the pony on the softest part of the road, managed to get past without attracting observation; and Jack soon rejoining him they proceeded on their way breathing rather more freely.

After a toilsome ascent they at length reached a lonely spot - a long strip of boggy land lying between the lower pasture lands and the higher moorlands. Here they halted, and releasing the pony of its load and securing it to a piece of grey rock, that rose up out of the ground, they went vigorously to work, and in a very short time had scooped out a grave in the peat bog, in which they deposited the sack and its contents, and lost no time in filling up the grave. By the time they had finished, twilight began to creep over the vast solitude around them. The storm had somewhat subsided. The clouds appeared watery, and lazily rolled about at a short distance above their heads, and altogether the scene presented to them was as gloomy and desolate as the most melancholy person could wish, Tom felt it to be congenial, but he felt, likewise, that it would not be safe to tarry there. After doing all that he possibly could to prevent any trace being left off their night's work, he untied the pony, and, giving it into the charge of Jack, ordered him off home by a circuitous route, and told him to get to Grassington as soon and as carefully as possible. Tom only tarried until he had driven his spade into the peat-bog with a piece of rock, and then hastily and stealthily preceded homeward by another path.

And was Tom Lee easier after having this successfully removed his victim's remains from the cave to the peat-bog? Perhaps he was a little relieved from the pressing fears and anxiety which he had lately so poignantly suffered, but not for long, for he found that the blood of the murdered man cried as loud for revenge from the peat bog on the solitary moorland as it had done from the shades of Grass Wood or the dark cave in the rocky Glen.

CHAPTER V   STRONGER SUSPICIONS STILL

The disappearance of Dr Petty remained as much a mystery as ever. Notwithstanding every means being used to obtain intelligence of the missing man, still nothing could be heard of him. Whether he was living or dead, no one with absolute certainty could say. Some few inclined to the opinion that he had decamped from the neighbourhood under the pressure of circumstances, the nature of which would later be revealed, but the majority felt fully persuaded that either some accident had happened to him, or he had met with foul treatment at the hands of some unknown, and in the minds of these, as we have before observed, suspicion pointed to Tom Lee. As it merely suspicion, however, with the exception of one here or there, such as Dick Linton, most people were very wary in giving utterance of their opinions on the subject.

The strongest feelings of curiosity to know the cause of the doctor's sudden disappearance prevailed throughout the district, but far stronger feelings possessed the breasts of those who were more nearly concerned in the matter. There was one who endured all the torturing agony of suspense. In vain did Mrs Petty try to imagine the cause of her husband's absence. The more she thought about it, the more she was at a loss to divine the cause. That he stayed away from the house voluntarily she could not for a moment bring herself to believe; for never was there a kinder or more considerate husband, or a more tender or loving father than the doctor; but if the act was not voluntary, what detained him?

This question continually suggested itself to her excited mind, and was followed by the gloomiest apprehensions. Who can describe the feelings of those who thus bereft of the dearest object of their deep and affectionate regard? In such circumstances, to know the worst is easier to bear than the intense agony which uncertainty produces in the mind. Imagination seizes the reins of empire, and rules every thought and feeling. The vivid and ever-changing pictures it presents agitates the mind with forebodings of undefined and alarming ills. If the foreground be lighted up with a single gleam of light, the background is dark and obscure; And as the eye in vain endeavours to pierce the gloomy maze, the soul is filled with dread, the spirits sink, and the bitterest misery ensues. Such was the state of mind to which the doctor's wife was reduced as day after day passed away and no intelligence of her absent partner could from any source be had. Her agony of mind soon made inroad on her physical strength. As we have already said, she became seriously ill, and was reduced to such a state of mental depression physical frustration, that her life was despaired of by those who gently tended her in her unhappy circumstances.

Few weeks after the disappearance of the unfortunate Dr, and towards the close of a cheerful winter's day, old Robert stood in the stable doorway, with one foot on the low step and the other on the pavement of the yard, holding the door with one hand in an apparently hesitating attitude. Now he looked wistfully at old Dobbin, having just given him a fresh supply of sweetly scented hay, and then looked towards the surgery door, evidently expecting the arrival of someone. His countenance was sad. The lines of his face were harder drawn. His hollow eye, the prominent cheekbone marked with a few streaks of the vermilion tint, so characteristic of the aged rustic labour, and the whole expression of his features told of the great anguish of mind which he had lately and was then suffering. He was as puzzled as ever to account for his master's absence.

"Where can he be, and what can he be doing?" asked he of himself.

He had asked this question hundreds of times, and had failed as often to frame a satisfactory answer.

"It cannot be because there's ought wrong between him an' th' missus – I never saw a single sign o' that in my life. It cannot be because he were short o' brass, because I ken he's some at bank; an' I'se sure it cannot be because there were ought wrong between him an' me, for he's never given a wrong word all th' time I've been wi' him. God bless him wherever he is. I cannot bide to think about it; It'll knock me right up, it will." And the old man's mouth puckered up and his eyes rolled in his head as if they were determined to keep something back that were as determined to make their appearance; but it was no use, he gave way, and the big teardrops rolled down his aged cheeks indicative of the deep trouble of his heart.

"An' it's likely to be the end of th' missus, too, it is," continued he, as he brushed the tears away from the fustian sleeve of his striped waistcoat, "but I'll go and see how she is, I will."

He was pulling to the door when Dobbin gave a hearty neigh. "Hear ye there, now, but it does me good to hear that, th' brute's like as if he knew that th' master's away; he's like me, he sadly wants him back again," and Robert went to reciprocate what he considered to be dobbin's love for his master, by tenderly patting the beast's neck, and in the excitement of the moment he lustily shouted out, "Where is he?" Dobbin again neighed, but there was no other answer to the troubled cry of the old man. Giving the horse another pat, and doing his best to remove all traces of his emotions, he left the stable and went to inquire after his mistress. Opening the kitchen door, he found Nelly sitting by the fire, stopping as if her heart was breaking.

Nelly sobbed, "Oh, Robert, I'se feared it'll be too much for the 'missus. Mrs Nightlamp's just been down, and she says as how Dr Diddlegan says she's very bad. And she keeps crying out for th' master. Oh, what's to become of the children, if ought should happen to her?"

"Nowt Is going to happen to her," returned Robert testily, but the very thought of such a thing was more than he could bear. "I don't ken what ye wimmin is made of - you can peel a onion, but ye must blubber and cry. Ye says she's poorly; I've not one to deny it; but for that matter ye'll no need to take on that way, as if th' world were at an end."

"Oh! Ye're an unfeeling man! If ye'd gotten wed like other folk, ye'd have a more feeling for folk than ye have, ye would – talking that way when missus is so bad."

"I'se as much feeling as thee, anyhow; there's oft the most feeling where there's least showing; But it's no use talking to the. As Dick Linton called at the surgery yet?"

"No," bawled out Nelly, considerably nettled at the insinuation that a sympathy with her mistress was not sincere.

"What sort of an answer's that, I should like to know?" asked Robert, feeling that he had gone rather too far, but not liking to show it.

"Why, it's as good as ye gets anyhow. I feel for th' missus as much as ye do," answered Nelly.

"Well, maybe ye do, but let me know if th' missus gets worse," said Robert as left the kitchen.

"Ye'll have to mend your manners if I do," bawled out Nelly, as old Robert shut the door, "I wish ye were wed, I do, ye'll never come to yer senses till ye are."

Robert made no reply, but sauntered into the lane leading to Coniston, in a very uneasy state of mind. Coming to a gate leading into a field, he leaned over it, and was soon lost deep in thought; and now and then soliloquizing.

"Well Robert, how ye getting on? Ye look fearful glum. Have ye heard ought o' th' doctor yet?" It was Dick Linton who addressed him, having come up a pathway through the fields below, and came suddenly upon old Robert and put an end to his soliloquy.

I'm gloomy enough and I think there's a reason. Missus is at death's door and as for th' doctor I've nearly cracked my brain wi' thinking about him. Has thou heard ought on him?"

"Not I," said Dick, "and I'll tell you what I think, he'll do no more good in this world, neither for his wife nor anybody else."

"What does thou mean?" enquired Robert, his lips trembling as he asked.

"I mean that ye'll never see him alive again, so dunnat expect it. Whether he's at bottom o' th' Wharfe or buried somewhere in th' neighbourhood, I don't pretend to say, but I cannot help thinking that he's dead."

"Thou doesn't say so, does thou?" interrogated Old Robert with a tremulous voice.

"I do," answered Dick, becoming a little excited, "I do, an' I'll stand it, or ye may call me too-late-for-the-dinner. And I've reason," continued he, "didn't I hear that Tom Lee (oh, he's a gallows-looking thief an' he's never hardly out o' my mind) threaten the doctor's life, an' my own too, at old Dame Hodgson's at Kilnsey – an' weren't th' doctor missing th' same night? And didn't Jerry Fenton an' them find traces of blood in

Grass Wood th' morning after? An' didn't the glass fall to the floor without breaking? See ye, Bobby, Tom Lee has as sure done for th' doctor as there's water in the Wharfe,", and with this clincher he took hold of the old man's arm, and said, "Is that young Diddlegan that's doing duty for poor Petty in th' surgery? I'se just let him look at my thumb, an' then I'se going up into town to see what's afresh."

"Is thee thumb no better then?" asked Robert as they proceeded towards the surgery.

"Yes, it's a deal better, but I cannot use my hand much yet. Wait about a bit, I'se not be long afore I'm with ye," and Dick went into the surgery.

Old Robert felt more than ever depressed after Dick had delivered himself so confidently as to the fate of his master, and bitter were his feelings as he contemplated his future prospects in the gloaming of that winter's evening, for next to the deep sorrow he felt for his master and the family - the reflection that the comfortable bread of his old age would, in all probability, be cut off, that he would have to find out other means to secure a livelihood, perhaps among strangers, was to him a truly sorrowful one. His reflections, however, were soon put to an end, for Dick soon rejoined him and they both proceeded up into the village in earnest conversation. Sauntering up the 'town-gate' they met a number of miners returning from their day's toil.

Among them was Jim Brown who, recognising Dick, at once saluted with him, "Well Dick, how is thou? I haven't seen thee this age of a duck," and seeing his arm slung, continued, "What's thee been up to now? Another drunken stir, I'll be bound."

"Nay, thou's wrong this time," returned Dick, "I strained my thumb a bit t'other day when I slipped, that's all."

"Thou aren't a lucky fellow – there's always summat happening, but I say, Dick, they tell me that thou knows summat about the doctor, is it true? I should like to hear what's become of him fearful well."

"And so should we all," chimed in two or three of his companions.

"Nay, I know nowt but what any child may know, if they'll no but use their wits," said Dick. "Ye all know what sort of chap that Tom Lee is. And ye know as well as I do about his threatenings, as I've been saying just now to old Robert here. I know all these things an' I tell my mind; but it's perilous speaking it – folk are so mealy mouthed now-a-days. I'se sure Tom has summat to do wi' it; but it you don't mind, we'll go and get a pint at th' Blue Anchor, an' see how Tom carries his self."

They all agreed to Dick's proposition, and at once repaired to Tom's house. On entering the kitchen they passed Tom's wife, who was just going out, and found

Tom sat on one side of the fire-place, smoking his pipe, and Jack Sharp sat at the table-end, eating an early supper.

"Tom, what's fresh?" enquired Dick, as he sat down, but Tom answered not, for at the sight of Dick, his conscience was up in arms, and the sudden motion of his heart communicated itself to his lips, which quivered with subdued rage, for Dick Linton was the last man he would have welcomed to his house. Having frequently heard of Dick's outspoken opinions respecting Dr Petty's disappearance, he hated and feared him more than any other person. Policy, however, kept him from any undue manifestations of his feelings, and he assumed as easy and careless a demeanour as he possibly could under the circumstances.

"What! Has thou bad blood in thee yet? Will ye not speak? I'm a bit of a strackle-brain myself, but I'll never bear malice as long as t' blood runs up an' down my body,", and, whistling, he shouted, "Bring me a quart o' ale, Dame, will ye? Nay, I'll pay for it, Jim," continued he, on seeing the person addressed bring out an old greasy purse, "I'll pay. Will any of thee smoke? I say, Missus, let's have an half-an-ounce of baccy at the same time, will ye?"

Upon being supplied with tobacco and ale, they all fell to smoking and drinking in silence. Jack Sharp, before he had finished his meal, made his exit, for his conscience was made of different stuff to Tom's, and not liking such close facility to Dick Linton, and fearing either by look or word to give any signs as to the true state of matters, and the bring on himself the vengeance which his master had often threatened him with, did he divulge the fearful secret locked up in the innermost steps of his mind, he thought they had better have his room and his company. They sat in silence some time, but that was a state of things quite foreign to Dick Linton's taste and nature. He therefore broke the silence.

"Is there ought fresh stirring in Grassington?" enquired he towards Jim Brown, at the same time closing one eye, "it's no use asking Tom there; he looks as foul as thunder about summat."

"Nowt as I knows," answered Jim, and he returned Dick's wink, continued, "we can think about nowt else but Dr Petty. There's a regular hullabaloo about him. He were a regular gentleman; an' none of you stuck-up animals can look sideways at a poor man for your starched-up sideboards. We all liked him, didn't we, Harry?" continued he, addressing one of his companions, "I wonder where in the world he is?"

"What thinks you, Jim, if we all guess round where he is? We can happen make summat out," said Dick, "an' I propose that Tom over there guesses first? Tom, we're waiting."

"You won't be waiting long here, if ye dunnat shut up," said Tom, with a flashing eye, at the same time moving about uneasily in his chair, for he felt that Dick had a design in putting the question, and his rising ire was with the greatest difficulty suppressed.

"Why, cannot a man put a civil question? And in a public house an' all. Thou art fearful touchy nowadays, thou must hav' murdered somebody."

"If thou doesn't shut up, I'll tell thee, and by thy own business, I'll murder thee, ye swilling-tub," said Tom, seizing a huge poker, and brandishing it over Dicks head with menacing fury. "Thy tongue was fearful loose up at Kilnsey, but it might not wag here."

"Why, what have I said to nettle thee so, if your conscience's all right for such a foul looking thief as thou art?" said Dick, instinctively rising at the same time in self-defence, and furious at Tom's threatening. "See thee, thou has threatened me oft before now, an' I haven't forgotten it neither; but I'll tell you this, I've the upper hand alright, I'd put an end to it now, I'd double thee up and make a wheelbarrow out of you, and roll thee down into the Wharfe and clear the countryside of its terror."

Tom was too enraged to answer Dick, but aimed a blow at his opponent's head. Jim Brown, seeing this, jumped up just in time to ward it off, or Dick would never have returned to Kilnsey alive.

"Now, now, Tom, what the deuce does though mean?" shouted Jim, as he wrenched the poker from the furious hand, "Thou must be ill at ease, or thou never would take on so, at what Dick said."

At this moment Tom's wife entered the room, attracted by the noise of the quarrel.

Tom, full of the most intense hatred for Dick Linton, and full of the most anxious fear of anything bubbling out respecting the doctor, thought it would be best to leave the room, lest something should occur in his house to strengthen the already strong suspicions of the whole village and surrounding district, of his connection with the affair. Ordering his spouse out of the room, therefore, he followed her without speaking another word to anyone, leaving the company to their newly replenished quart of ale.

"Now," said Dick to his companions, in an undertone, as soon as Tom had left them, "I think he'll be in my way of thinking afore long. If Tom's innocent, why does he make this stir?"

"Just so," said Jim Brown, "I begin to think that there's summat in it. Does thou know what I've heard today?"

"Nay – what has thou heard?" asked Dick.

"Why, thou knows old Peter Bentham, that lives up at that farm at th' moor-edge, doesn't thou?"

"Very well," answered Dick, "what of him?"

"Why, just this: th' night but one after the doctor went missing, Peter's wife were up late, for it were between two an' three in the morning, an' she heard horse's feet coming up th' lane below th' house, an' wondering who it could be at that time, she looked out th' corner of th' window, an' she saw somebody coming quietly up to th' door, and a bit behind 'em were somebody leading a grey pony on one side of th' road, with summat like a sack o' chips on its back, an' she could almost swear its was Tom's grey galloway. An' beside that, old Peter were up at th' moor, the morning after, and he traced the pony's foot-marks to a bog where there seemed to have been a deal o' trampling, and all about seemed as if there'd been some spadework going on. Now, what's to be made o' that? I tell thee what, Dick, I begin to be a bit o' the mind, and Tom's way tonight makes me more so."

"Oh, thing's will square themselves yet," said Dick, "but let's say no more about it. Sup up, Harry," said he to one of his drinking companions, at whom the glass stood, "an' let's be goin', for I must be up at Kilnsey by foddering time. Come, Bobby, is thou going down too?"

With this they departed, and I'm getting into the street Dick advised them all to keep a sharp lookout, a stiller tongue than he could do, and something would turn up sooner or later, then bidding each other good night they took their several ways.

But come with us, reader, into the back kitchen of the Blue Anchor Inn. What means the look of consternation depicted on the countenance of Tom Lee; those large drops of sweat which bead his brow – that fixed gaze into the dark red fire? What means the flushed face - the keen, restless look of Dame Lee? What means the waxen-looking chilly face; the trembling limbs of Jack Sharp? Simply the powerful workings of conscience in them all. They had overheard the conversation which a while before had taken place in their dwelling, and their feeling of security had crumbled atoms. There they sat, a dumb committee of ways and means to extricate themselves from their fearful forebodings, and to remove all chance of detection of their criminal proceedings. For some time fear returned to Dame Lee so briskly, that she could not retire to bed, for there's no sleep for those so paralysed that they cannot frame their thoughts and future plans into words. After sitting some time, however, turning things over in his own mind, Tom, to screw up his own courage, began to abuse his wife and Jack. Addressing the latter, he broke out with,

"What does thou sit there for trembling like a sneaking greyhound? Thou hasn't the heart of a hen, an' as for thee," continued he, addressing his dame, "thou sees what thy plan for taking th' sack up into the peat-bog is likely to come to. Away with thee to bed, for I've summat to do yet afore morning, if that chap (eyeing Jack severely) has any pluck in him."

"It was your plan as much as mine," returned Dame Lee briskly, "but I'se not goin' to bed, because whatever it'll be I'll take part in it."

Then they proceeded to lay down a plan which, if carried out, would, as they imagined, set their minds at rest, and remove all traces of their guilt.

******

The hour of one in the morning resounded from the old grey tower of Linton church throughout the silent vale. The night was frosty, the atmosphere was clear, and the heavens were cloudless. Countless stars lighted up the firmament on high, each telling of the boundlessness of the mighty universe and of the infinite power of the dread Creator. To gaze one hour at such a time on the midnight sky and offer our devotions, with the lamp of divine truth burning on the altar of a pure, loving heart (for yields such deep, quiet happiness as thousands who crowd the temples reared by man, and who worship by line and rule according to human creeds, seldom realise). But to speak a word of praise of nature to those who have made up their minds that two and two make four - who have exultingly passed *pons assinorum* in the land of quadrants, compasses, and actual demonstration - whose profound attainment in theology are such that nothing possible can be added thereto or taken there from, is to worship her and become guilty of idolatry, given up to grovelling superstition. Notwithstanding the crotchets of such, however, how grand and awe-inspiring is the magnificent and sublime aspect which nature presents on a night like this. As man rises in spirit-thought through the starry depths of heaven, finding out the dwelling place of the most High - wandering among its bright intelligences, and witnessing their glorious life - how he feels his insignificance, it was his worthlessness, and his dependence upon the almighty author of his being, and how he pants for a better life. But nature is too pure to hold communion with the guilty; they cannot bear her innocent gaze - it condemns, and they turn away from her path.

At the hour we have just named, Tom Lee again left his house. He was accompanied this time by his wife. The thing he again purposed to do was another removal of the doctor's remains. Jack Sharp could not screw his courage up to assist a third time in such an undertaking, such was the fright he had already experienced. Tom equally disliked the work, but it was imperatively necessary, so he thought, for it to be done; for, from what had been overheard that night, it was more than probable that some steps might be taken to trace out the reason for his pony being on the moor at such an untimely hour; and in doing that Petty's body might be found. There was no alternative but the removal of the body to a more safe resting-place, attended though it might be with the risk of being seen by someone. They managed, with great care, to leave the village unobserved by any of its inhabitants, and they proceeded along the lonely road leading to the moor in gloomy abstraction. Bitter were Tom's feelings, ignorant and hard and as he was, at the thought of his wife's being under the necessity of taking part in such work; but he consoled himself a little with the thought that there was no help for it. The deed had been done, and means must be taken to avoid its terrible consequences, this last thought was the all-absorbing one with his dame - though not guilty of the actual deed, she felt that, whether the law touched her or not, she would be indirectly involved in all its consequences, as well as her children. The magnificent forms of nature had no attractions for them. The everlasting hills rising in the obscurity of night shadows around them, as firmly fixed on their foundations as when first moulded and placed there by the hands of the omnipotent one, suggested no thought to their minds. The glorious sight of the star-gemmed heavens awakened no lofty aspirations in their hearts as nor did they hear the sound of the night-winds among the wooded hills, as if nature was bewailing their guilty and unhappy career, touched no sympathetic chord in their bosoms.

Onward they went to the accomplishment of their unnatural work. Avoiding every farmstead, they at length reached the bog. While his wife held the pony, Tom stripped off his overcoat, and searching about for the handle of the spade, which he had left when at the place before, he soon found it, and, drawing the implement forth, he began to scoop out the peat which covered the terrible treasure. He was not long before he came at it, and succeeded in dragging it onto a bed of ling, where it lay until he had filled up the unconsecrated grave. This in such a manner as not to attract the eye of the curious, with the assistance of his wife, he lifted the sack onto the back of the pony. Securing it there with a cord he had brought for the purpose, he again drove his spade into the soft peat bog, and, in silence, they preceded across the moor in the direction of Hebden with the silent dead. They went and, though far away from any human habitation, they scarcely dare breathe for fear of attracting observation. They felt that the risk they were running was great; though it was not probable that anyone would cross their path At such a time, yet it was just possible, and, seen in such a guise, with such a burden, and at such a place, they felt that the prevalent suspicion of their being connected with the affair would at once ripen into certainty, and perhaps lead to condemning evidence of their guilt.

Before them rose from a deep bed of heather a large grey moorcock, disturbed from his nest by their approach, and swept across the wide landscape. Tom, for a moment, dreadfully frightened, and pulling out from under his overcoat a huge bludgeon, put himself into an offensive attitude. Familiar with the sound, however, he soon made out the cause, and recovered himself immediately - it was his state of mind which had made a coward of him. His wife, though a woman of strong nerve, on hearing the noise gave a faint scream and sank to the ground.

"Oh, Tom, do not kill him!" said she, seeing his threatening attitude and weapon, "one's enough – oh! Who is it?"

"Shut up, you fool!" answered Tom sullenly, "an' get up. What's thou doing cowerin' down there for? It's only a moorcock. A bonnie one thou art to help somebody through this business. Thou art worse than Jack. If Jack had frightened me like that, I'd have knocked his head off."

"I thought it were somebody that you were going to hit with that stick," said the dame, reassured and rising from the ground.

"If there had been somebody there, thou'd a done for us with thy blind talk. It were one of them cursed moorcocks; if I had got it, I'd screw its neck round."

"Well, let's get down to the' Wharfe; I'se not be easy till we've gotten shot of our load," said the Dame, and by this time they had reached the edge of the moor overlooking Wharfedale, a little distance above the village of Burnsall. Descending warily down the rough hillside, down an uneven packhouse road, they came at length within sight and sound of the river at a point where the smooth surface of the water denoted that it was of considerable depth, they proceeded to relieve the pony of its burden.

As they neared the bank of the river, a young man might have been seen leaving the village of Burnsall a short distance below. Passing by the bridge which led over the Wharfe, he preceded a little higher up the opposite bank and crossed over the 'hipping-stones', being a shorter and more direct road to the village of Grassington, that being the place where he was bound. Reaching the other side, he posted on his way at a brisk pace, lost in pleasant dreams of love, for he had been on a courting expedition, and Cupid had been more than ordinary propitious on the occasion. Though the hour was late and the road lonely he had no fears - the tender yet earnest vows of unchanging affection breathed into his eager ear that night by the fair maid of Burnsall had set his heart all of a glow, and filled it with so much courage that had all the 'boggarts' of Wharfedale confronted him in one formidable phalanx, he would have forced his way through them as if they had been so many river reeds. A glorious vision of good things to come filled his imagination - he saw the church, he saw the parson, he heard the merry bells, he saw his lovely bride, and was just about to embrace her, when –

"Holloa, what's this?" said Ned Sykes to himself, on hearing a plunge in the river, at the same time halting and looking over a hedge which he had just passed in the direction whence the sound preceded. "Has somebody fallen in? If that isn't Tom Lee's Galloway pony, an' if that isn't Tom and his wife I'll be shot! Why, what in the world are they doing here at this time o' night?" As Ned thus soliloquised, he saw Tom Lee, his wife, and the pony ascending from the river's bank towards the road above. Having tied a large stone to the sack containing poor Petty's remains with the cord which had secured it to the pony's back, they rolled both into the river, but in the descent the stone slipped, unobserved by them, from the cord. After having thus accomplished their purpose they immediately left the place, and returned to Grassington by the same road they had come, thinking it more safe than going along the public highway. As they retreated, Ned advanced to the spot, but nothing could he see that in the least indicated what had been the object of such a visit - the doctor's body had sunk to a temporary resting-place under the river's sedgy bank, and its surface reflected the light of the solemn stars as if it had never been disturbed.

"By-the-heart!" but this licks me – it does!" What can they want here at this time of the night; and I could have almost sworn it were Tom and the wife, said Ned Sykes, having forgotten everything about brides, weddings, and wedding bells, trudged away to

Grassington, wondering much about the strange event he had just witnessed.

CHAPTER VI   A DISCOVERY

Calmly the morning broke over hill and dale. The forehead of the mighty sun appeared above the tips of the mist-veiled eastern mountains, and he shook from his flaming locks the golden light and scattered it over the bosom of nature as she awoke from her night's repose. Silently the light spread over the far extended scene - creeping into quiet glens, and by the side of purling rills which fed on their way green bright looking water cresses, little thriving colonies of which had located themselves in the various pleasant sequestered places of Wharfedale - filled the purple heather bells on the moorland, and sparkling in the myriad dewdrops which covered the high pasturelands where struggling sheep nibbled among the frosted grass or the turnips with which their thoughtful shepherd had provided them. The woods were nearly stripped of their summer dress, only retaining a few red leaves to cover their nakedness, and their tangled brushwood and gnarled arms were exposed to the rude blasts of winter. The loving cattle, the cock's shrill clarion, and the barking of the shepherd's cur from the mountains, sounded through the veil, the inhabitants of which began to address themselves to another day's duty.

It was Sabbath morn - a Sabbath morning in England - the land of the brave and the free! An English Sabbath morn in the country! A peaceful serenity brooded over the scene. Nature herself in calm repose seemed to show her frailty to the great Lord of the Sabbath. The robin carolled his morning song from the hawthorn spray overlooking the door of the farmstead, not far from which gurgled forth, from under the moss-covered orchard wall, a clear crystal spring which merrily danced away down by the meadow side, into the glen, and onward to the Wharfe. Cheerfully the household bird sang with a hopeful eye fixed up on the windowsill for his accustomed crumb. The rattling of milk-pails - the noise of the stalled cattle - the cackle of geese and fowls - the active preparations for the morning's repast going on in the large old fashioned kitchen - well stocked with hams, flitches, and brown Yorkshire oak cakes, all told of the well-to-do circumstances of the honest grey-headed old farmer whose boast is that he has never been in a Court of Justice - that he and his four elders have lived on the same farm for 200 years back - that he has always paid his rent at the time, that he has never once missed going to church every Sunday for the last thirty years, and that he does not intend to miss that morning.

The blue curling columns of smoke in the distance yonder - rising gently and gracefully through 'the air serene', shows where the village of Burnsall cosily nestles in the winding vale, and that its humble inhabitants are astir, too, and are preparing or partaking their frugal meal. And hark! Now the church gives forth its pleasant and tuneful voice, summoning the dwellers of the vale, far and near, from their home devotions to the public worship of the God of their fathers in the venerable church which stands near the river side. Here and there an aged pilgrim, staff in hand, wends slowly his way towards the sacred edifice with the eye of his mind turned down the pathway of life he has travelled, thinking of the joys of youth, the cares of life, and the rest before him, until reaching the kirk-yard he meets other aged friends, when sauntering among the tombstones, deciphering their inscriptions, he talks over with them the by-gone scenes and events of life. Groups of happy youth - handsome young men, and beautiful young maidens approach the same place exchanging hearty greetings of 'good mornings' and 'good wishes' mingled with arch looks, longing looks, and hopeful glances, which are destined to result in happy marriages and healthy promising progeny that will form the life, and conduct the future affairs, of the sequestered vale. And now the quickened tones of the bell announces the hour of service has arrived, when young and old enter the temple to pay the homage of their souls to the King of kings.

Sauntering along the Riverside a little below the church were two or three young villagers whiling away the time in idle gossip, and trying which could skim pebbles the farthest along the surface of the river.

"What's that, Bill?" asked one of his companions, whose eye had followed the pebble he had just flung across the river to the opposite bank, and had caught in the glance a floating object under the overhanging branches of some hazel trees which grew there. "I dunna ken," said Bill, "but it looks like a sack; let's go over to th' other side and see."

And away they went to make out what the object could be, loudly shouting in the excitement of the moment. Running towards the 'hipping stones' and having to pass near the church, they attracted the attention of old Peter Dawson, who combined in his proper person the official character of Sexton and verger, and who, in his own estimation at least, was a most important and ecclesiastical functionary. Standing in the church porch as the youths passed, and highly incensed at the impropriety of their conduct, he rushed forth, black rod in hand, to command peace. But the young man, having got part of the way across the river, did not heed his commands - on they went till they reached the object of their curiosity. They managed to draw it to the banks of the river, but on one of them perceiving a human foot protruding from the sack, they are suddenly took to their heels in the direction they had come. Peter Dawson was there to receive them, and intended the reception to be a warm one, but such was their terror that they regarded him no more than if he had been the mile-stone that stood in the highway above. Peter brandished his rod of office over the head of the first who re-crossed the river, and was about to smite the Sabbath-breaker and peace-disturber, when the delinquent stammered out, "Peter, there's a drowned man in a sack at th' other side."

The rod fell harmlessly.

"What does thou say?" asked Peter, scarcely believing the statement, but somewhat taken aback by the terror-stricken countenance of the youths. They all confirmed the assertion of their spokesman.

"Go back wi' me, an' let's see what we can make of it," said Peter, to put the truth of their statement to the test. Away they went, but great was Peter surprised to find they had told the truth. They proceeded to remove the sack and examine the body to ascertain its personality. Peter looked long and carefully, and at last seemed to come to a certain conclusion in his own mind with which he acquainted those who accompanied him no more than by saying, partly to himself, "Oh, th' secret's out at last," and away he strode in the direction of the church followed by the young men who wondered much as to his intentions. On reaching the church door he bade them remain in the porch, and immediately disappeared behind the green baize covered inner door. On entering the nave of the church, the first pew he came to was that in which were sat the constable of the district and the churchwardens, before whom, in imposing array, gaudily-painted staves and other insignia of office, were conspicuously placed. He communicated his intelligence to them, and being in an excited state of mind, what he communicated was partly overheard by others that sat nearby.

"A man found drowned. It's Doctor Petty," ran like lightning round the church. After a short earnest conversation the officials seized their staves and immediately left their pew. Others followed - and still others, until in a very short time nearly the whole congregation had gone to the banks of the Wharfe. Old Parson Alcock, who had just begun a discourse from the sixth commandment, looked round in astonishment on the conduct of his hearers, and was about to make some severe comments there on, when the clerk, leaving his desk, ascended to that of the preachers and explained to him the cause of the strange proceedings.

"Doctor Petty's found!" shouted the now excited Parson, and closing his book he at once followed after his runaway flock, with the remainder at his heels. On reaching the spot where the body lay, he found Andrew Bland, the constable, closely questioning the young men who first saw it, as to how they got it out, or if they had disturbed it in any way. Peter Dawson removed the sack so far as to enable him to identify the remains, but nothing more. Satisfied that nothing else had been done, he told them their presence and evidence would be required at the inquest. He then had the body removed to the Bridge Tavern - sent for the coroner of the district, and made all the arrangements necessary for the inquest being held the next day. The whole village was aroused. This would also have been the case if the body found had been unknown, but being recognised as the Doctor's (and there was no difficulty in identifying it, for having been buried in the peat-bog, it was not decomposed in the least - the features were perfect, excepting a few bruises about the head) the greatest excitement prevailed.

One part of the mystery of his disappearance was now partly made out – the doctor had not decamped from the neighbourhood as some had supposed, - and nothing conceivable could have led him to commit suicide, - and if not, then murder it seems had been committed. If so, then by whom? And for what cause? Speculation was at its height. People put this and that together and made out a case, and almost every group made out a different one - different in its particulars, but all agreeing as to the fact of murder having been perpetrated; and their deductions from foregones led to a pretty general unanimity of opinion, though carefully expressed, as to the perpetrator of the deed. They all hoped that fresh light would be thrown on that part of the mystery during the inquest the following day. The parson said a few appropriate words to them under the circumstances - counselled them not to rashly condemn anyone, but leave all in the hands of Providence, who would sooner or later clear away all the mystery which hung about the affair; and putting them in mind of the sacredness of the day, he wished them quietly to disperse and calmly await the results of the inquest.

In the meantime, Andrew Bland having heard of what Ned Sykes had seen on the previous evening, thought it was his duty to go to Grassington and have an interview with him, as his evidence at the inquest might be of importance. Another object he had in view, too, in going was to break the intelligence to the doctor's wife. On going over the bridge at the foot of the hill on which the village of Grassington stands, he made a full stop, and leaning over the battlement of the bridge, gazing into the boiling waters as they rushed through its arches, he began to cast about in his mind the best way of breaking the sad news to Mrs Petty. He knew from hearsay that she had recovered a little strength of body, and under the buoying feeling of hope - that good angel who is the last to desert the distressed - she had meekly bowed her head and taken up her cross. The torture of suspense had given way to a feeling of resignation to the Divine will - her eye of faith had caught, in its searchings into the mystery of the severe dispensation, the golden entrance leading to a place of security, both for herself and her children, even the tender pity and promised protection of the husband of the widow and father of the fatherless, with whom alone can there be found for anyone, in any kind of trouble, that succour which has tried humanity at times, so much needs.

"I'se frightened of throwing her again," said old Andrew to himself, perplexed what plan to adopt, "an' they tell me that she's getting' over her troubles a bit. I think in my mind I'd better see Mr Diddlegan about it, and tell him to break the news as nicely as he can tell her. He'll manage it as well as anybody, 'cause he knows her situation and what she can bide and all about it, I'll be bound."

Having come to this resolution, the constable started up the hill side towards Grassington, before reaching the village he turned up a green narrow lane which led to Mrs Petty's residence without going through the village. On reaching the backyard he saw an aged person standing in the kitchen doorway, and heard voices in altercation. "Ye'll never do as I want ye. It'll do you no harm to serve the canary now and then, for the master's sake; but it's 'out of sight out of mind', you'll like as if ye didn't care for him," said the old man standing with his hand on the door handle to someone inside.

"I care for him as much as ye do, anyhow," answered a shrill voice from within, "but ye've as much time as I have to serve it, I've the house to look after, and children to mind. Ye should have married like I said."

When Nelly (for it was she) got nettled, she always reminded old Robert of the serious mistake he made when young, of not getting married, and attributed it all to that lamentable fact in his history, all the little bits of irascible ebullitions of temper which he occasionally manifested. This the old man could not stand, and Nelly knew it right well.

"Ye're a ne'er-do-well, that's what ye are," said Robert, and pulling the door to rather smartly he went down the yard.

"Well Bobby, is that ye?" said Andrew Bland, meeting him.

"Aye, for sure it is. Who else could it be?" said Robert, snappishly, and, on looking up into the stranger's face, continued, "and who art thou? What, Andrew, is it thee? What are thee doing at Grassington today?"

"There's news about the doctor," answered Andrew.

"Thou doesn't say true, does thou?" asked Robert, brightening up.

"True enough," sighed Andrew, "but it's bad news."

"What is it?" Earnestly enquired Robert. "Oh, what is it?"

"His body has been taken out of th' Wharfe today."

Old Robert fixed his eyes on the constable. But spoke not. His cheek blanched - his lips trembled - he essayed to speak, but for some time he could not. Such was the effect of the sad intelligence upon him that he would have fallen to the ground had he not leaned against the wall near which he was standing for support.

"I'm sorry to trouble you so, Robert, but I've just told ye the truth, hard as it is to bear. There's been more hearts pained today - I'll assure ye. I've seen a deal o' full hearts an' wet cheeks. Everyone seems to be troubled about it; and how I'm to break it to Mrs Petty I do not know."

CHAPTER VII   NOT PROVEN

A little above Kilnsey, and not far from the Wharfe, stood a snug farm-stead, whose well cultivated fields stretched away to the river's brink. It seemed the abode of rustic contentment. Early on the following morning, a person with a lantern in one hand, and a large milk can in the other, issued from the house and proceeded with hurried steps across the farmyard towards the cow house. Morning was just breaking. The trees on the hill tops threw out their naked arms, and stood clearly defined against the light streak to the sky. Through one of these the morning star twinkled brilliantly, and attracted the eye of the farmer, who, after gazing on it awhile exclaimed,

"Oh, it's bonny! I wonder now if we've to live again after it's over with us here. I'm proud of old Wharfedale – it's grand to live among these hills. Hear ye what sweet music the river sings. When I look around at such a time as this, dang it, but it makes me as tender-hearted as a child – that's a summat that I could never right understand. I wonder if it's nature that wants to make me a better man - it makes me feel that I'm far frae being what I should be. I wouldn't change shoes with Tom Lee anyhow. I wonder if it's true that they've found the poor doctor."

And Dick Linton (for it was he) went into the mistral to milk the kine. After doing this he carried the milk into the kitchen, and was returning to fodder the cattle when he was accosted by Ned Sykes, who had then dropped into the yard.

"Get ready, Dick, as soon as ye can, an' go wit' me."

"What's up now?" asked Dick, at once recognising Sykes.

Ned at once told him that he had been sent up by Andrew Bland, and related all that had happened during the last few days in the neighbourhood of Burnsall, and that Dick was to go down and attend the inquest that day.

"Well, I bless my britches, if it isn't just working round as I always expected it would," exclaimed Dick, "I heard a bit of a wind on it last night, and I was getting ready to come down to see if there were any truth in the report. Come go get a bit of breakfast wi' me an' we'll go down together." So saying, Dick, after foddering his cattle, took Ned to join him in his mornings repast, consisting of oatmeal porridge and some new milk, which Dick called a "poultice for the stomach", asseverating, "that doctor had no chance, which folk had supposed and such like." They soon finished their meal, and, after Dick had given directions for the work of the day to his eldest son, they took the road to Kilnsey. On reaching Kilnsey, Dick proposed calling for a few minutes at the Angler's Inn, just to let the old couple know what had happened.

On entering the kitchen, they found 'mine host' sat in an old arm-chair by the fire-side, having placed his broad brimmed hat on the floor by the side of the chair, ready to begin his breakfast as soon as his good Dame, who was superintending the frizzling of a little home-fed bacon before the bright red fire, had completed her arrangements.

"Hello, Anthony, ye're ready I see for doing your duty," cried Dick, pointing to the dripping bacon, and seating himself on the end of the old, polished oak long settle, "missus, let's have a pint o' ale," continued he, addressing his hostess.

"Ye're beginning so early on in th' day, Dick," said the Dame on looking up from the collops she was just turning, and seeing who the customer was, "but maybe ye're off somewhere, said she," enquiringly.

"I'se been to Burnsall, wi' Ned here. Haven't ye heard what's up?"

"Why, old Jessop were here last night, an' he said summat about them havin' found th' doctor," said old Anthony. "Is there ought in it?"

"It's true enough," said Dick, just as Dame Hodgson brought in the ale.

"Ye dunnot say so, Dick?" asked she in an excited tone.

"I'll see ye both at the inquest I expect," said Ned.

"Now, ye've oft told me to keep my own counsel about it, missus," said Dick, "but ye see how nicely things are working round; see ye, I bear Tom Lee no malice, not a smite, for all the devil-skin he is, an' he's threatened me afore now, I'll always say, an' I'll stick to it yet, that it's nobody but Tom. And if it is, it'll come out some way or another. Lee'll get found out yet."

"That's right enough, Dick, but let it work round itself, and don't go and burn your finger wi' talking so fast," said the dame.

"I'se tell th' truth when it comes to it, an' maybe ye'll have to tell 'em what ye knows too, I shouldn't wonder," said Dick, as he rose to depart and, followed by Ned Skyes, he left the Angler's Inn and proceeded towards Burnsall.

The inquest on Dr Petty was to be held at the Bridge Tavern. The coroner having arrived the night before, had taken all the steps necessary to secure, as far as possible, evidence to prove satisfactorily the cause of the doctor's death; and, on the strengths of the reports he had heard, he had thought it his duty to have Tom Lee arrested as being implicated more or less in the foul play by which, to all appearance, the doctor had come to his sudden end. Accordingly, Tom was already in the custody of Andrew Bland in a backroom of the inn. The jurymen having been sworn, the coroner proceeded at once to take evidence, and called for Mr Richard Linton, but such was the rush and crush of the crowd eager to hear the examination of the witnesses, that the witnesses could not get into the room with the jury already sat, and nothing could be done. The coroner commanded the passage to be at once cleared, which was at length affected, and again he called aloud for the first witness, Mr Richard Linton. Just as Dick entered the room. "Here I am, yer honor, but plain Dick would have done. I want no handle to my name, I'se tell truth just same wi' being called Dick as Mr Richard."

"You have not come to indulge in irrelevant remarks," said the coroner, "but to answer the questions put to you."

"Well, well, I'm ready," said Dick.

"Then be pleased to tell what you know touching the death of the doctor."

Dick at once proceeded to tell what took place at the Angler's Inn - how Tom was the terror of the neighbourhood - how he bullied everyone who came in his way - how everyone suspected him of nefarious practises of different kinds - of house breaking and the like, and also of having attempted to rob one of the clerks of the lead mines on the highway - how in that attempt he was worsted and severely wounded, and had to go to Dr Petty to have his wound healed and how, consequently, Dr Petty was put into the secret - how like a madman he conducted himself at Anthony Hodgkin's - how the doctor checked him there, and reminded him of the secret he, the doctor, possessed - how Tom was exasperated thereat - how he threatened, in the presence of Dame Hodgson and himself, that he would do for the doctor and how he had no more doubt that Tom Lee had murd____

"Hold there," interposed the coroner, hastily, "you have no right whatever to give utterance to any such like opinion about any man before the man's guilt is proven; have you anything more to say?"

"No, I cannot say that I have, but if what I have said isn't enough, there is them that'll say more," said Dick as he left the room, under the firm conviction that there was evidence sufficient among the witnesses to hang Tom - consummation which he thought was devoutly to be wished.

The next witness called was Dame Hodgson, who had been brought to give her evidence, as it was deemed important that her testimony with regard to the threatening language which Tom had uttered at her house against the doctor should be taken. She fully corroborated Dick Linton's depositions, but added nothing more to incriminate Tom.

Jerry Fenton then deposed that he was one of the scouring party who went out to search for the doctor the day after he was missing, and that going through Grass Wood, he lighted upon a spot where the ground and brushwood all about had every appearance of a recent struggle having taken place, and that at one spot in particular the ground was covered with blood, and that, could the truth be come at, it was his strong belief that the doctor had met with his death blow in that wood. The coroner again objected to any private opinion being given before that of the jury had been pronounced. This witness having nothing more to depose, he made way for Jim Brown, the Grassington miner, who said that being at Tom Lee's house, the Blue Anchor, a night or two after the doctor had so mysteriously disappeared, in company with Dick Linton and a few more, the all-engrossing subject was muted in Tom's presence, and the question being put to him by Dick, relative to the doctor's whereabouts, he seemed to be uncommonly ill at ease - too much so for an innocent man -and was so infuriated that he had once made a murderous attack upon Dick with the fire poker, and undoubtedly would have killed him on the spot had no one interfered to ward off the dreadful blow aimed at him; and if Tom had been innocent of the crime he was so generally supposed suspected of, it was his opinion_____

"Hold on there," again vociferated the coroner, "how many times am I to repeat that we won't know opinions here, we want evidence bearing upon the case in hand have you any more to adduce?" He received a reply in the negative.

"The next witness," he cried out, "bring the next witness in, Mr Bland," addressing the constable.

Dame Bentham from the moor-edge farm, above Grassington, then deposed that the night but one after the doctor was missing, or rather it was between two and three o'clock in the morning, she had not retired to bed, being engaged in some particular household duties, when she heard the approach of horse along the road leading close past the house, and, looking out of the window, she saw a man stealthily creeping towards the house door at the same time, and on the further side of the road, was another man leading a grey galloway pony with something like a sack of potatoes on its back. As soon as the galloway had gone past, the man left the door, and the thought struck her that he had been holding the door for fear of someone coming out and seeing who they were that were passing at that time of night. Now she was certain that the pony was Tom Lee's, for she had seen it hundreds of times before, and she felt no doubt, though he was disguised, that it was Tom who led it, and that his errand up there at that untimely hour was for no good purpose. She further deposed that her husband, out of curiosity at such an unusual thing, went on to the moor above the following morning, and saw above the peat bog, on close inspection, every indication of something having been buried there. This was the amount of her evidence.

The next witness called was Ned Sykes, who said that coming home from Burnsall to Grassington, a few nights back (naming the night) he had just crossed the 'hipping stones' over the Wharfe and was walking along at a brisk pace when he heard a splash in the river, and looking over the hedge, he saw to his astonishment, Tom Lee, with his wife and Tom's grey pony, all ascending the bank of the river. He was certain it was them, for the night was frosty and very star-light, and that he did not entertain the slightest doubt as to their identity - he went to the place immediately after they had gone to try an account for their being at that place at that time of night - he looked into the river, but could see nothing - he went home wondering what could be the cause of their visit, and when the doctor's body was found near the place, he had communicated what he had seen to the constable, feeling persuaded in his own mind that Tom Lee's visit there had something to do with the matter in some way or other.

This completed the evidence, and the coroner preceded at once to sum up. In his remarks to the jury he said that there was the greatest difficulty, in cases like the one upon which they had met to consider, to view matters in an unbiased light. Men's feelings and prejudices were in general so strong that it often required a stronger effort to form a just and deliberate opinion on the evidence adduced - the more so as very often the evidence itself was of a conflicting nature. In the evidence given to them that day there had been no lack of positive imputation, which lead them, were they not very careful, to presume guilt where guilt could not be proved. In the evidence given by the witness Linton they would observe that certainly a motive was presented to them for Lee's perpetrating such a deed, as conveyed in the threatening language he used on that occasion.

The fact of the doctor's never being seen again after leaving Kilnsey that night strengthened such a supposition. Then the evidence of Fenton's finding marks of a violent scuffle and traces of blood on the road by which the doctor must necessarily have come from Kilnsey in returning home, favoured the supposition still more. Then the testimony of the witness Peter Bentham, who saw Tom and his pony with a sack on its back passing along such an out-of-the-way road at such an untimely hour, might very easily lead them to suspect that the doctor's remains were being conveyed to some secret place - the more so as those remains were eventually found in a sack. Then another link in the chain of evidence which favoured the supposition that Lee was guilty of the deed was found in the testimony of the witness Sykes, who saw, as you are aware, Tom, his wife, and the pony, on the bank of the Wharfe at the very spot where the body was afterwards found - who heard a plunge into the river of what? Was it Petty 's body? Of this there was no direct proof. However mysterious, and even suspicious, Lee's movements had been, his opinion was that there was no positive proof that Lee was the perpetrator of the horrible crime of murder - circumstantial evidence was strongly against him, but actual proof that he had done the deed, he was of the opinion that there was none. If they too thought so after due deliberation, their duty, of course, would be to acquit the prisoner. The jury, who then retired for a considerable time, acquitted the prisoner.

Tom Lee, who had been present during the investigation, and who had sat all the time in sullen silence, regarding the several witnesses as they appeared with a calm look of defiance (which, however, was far from being real) - on hearing the verdict, at once got up without manifesting the slightest emotion of any kind, and made for the door accompanied by the constable. He had no thoughts but of being set at liberty forthwith, and his intention was to post away to Grassington to inform his wife, who from movements of policy had kept away, of the fortunate turn matters had taken. But he was greatly disappointed in this, for no sooner had he skipped the passage than, by order of one of the Skipton magistrates, he was taken again into custody, and as soon as he had taken a little refreshment was conveyed to Skipton.

The reason for this was a strong feeling of dissatisfaction at the result of the inquiry at the inquest on the part of some influential inhabitants of the district. Not only did the lower classes entertain strong conviction of Tom's guilt, but all grades, up to the highest, felt persuaded in their minds of his criminality, and those who knew him the best and were most acquainted with his antecedents were loudest in their assertions of his guilt. Among these none were more dissatisfied with the verdict the jury had given than Tobias Sedgwick, a most worthy magistrate of the Skipton bench. He was a fine specimen of the old-fashioned Tory, was Tobias, such as lived in the days of yore, but who are fast dying out - he was as blue as indigo, as honest and straightforward as Washington and as hearty, kind, and jovial as old Christmas. But though he praised those who did well in life, he was a regular terror to evil-doers. He could not but think that if the case were taken into the Magistrates Court at Skipton something more could be elicited that would lead to the conviction of Tom Lee; not that he desired such a termination of the matter from any particular personal dislike he felt for Tom, but a sense of duty, as a magistrate who had the well-being of all around him at heart, led him to make the most active assertions to come to the root of the matter. If Tom proved innocent he would rejoice as much as anyone at his acquittal, but if guilty then he would with little pity hand him over to the tender mercies of the law, and rid the district of one who had been its terror for many years. He had principally been induced to try the case at Skipton and, from having been told by the head constable of that place that if the prisoner was remanded for a week he, the constable, thought he could bring evidence forward that would lead to Tom's conviction, as he had received some very important information or the inquest was being held. Old Betty Knowle, a pot-hawker, a person well known in the neighbourhood, had had some conversation with Jack Sharp, up at Litton, which left no doubt upon her mind that Tom Lee had more or less been mixed up in the affair. She had been led to give the information on account of some ill-treatment she had received at the hands of Tom Lee, in years gone by, and the nature of the conversation would transpire when the case came on at Skipton.

As soon as Tom Lee heard of the doctor's body having been found, he felt that the time had come when all the iron nerve and fearlessness of the consequences of what he did, which he generally was master of, would be needed, and he braced himself up for all possible contingencies. The first thing he did was to get rid of Jack Sharp for a while, until the storm that was brewing had passed by. From the state of fear in which Jack continuously was, he thought it would be best to get him away from the immediate neighbourhood, and arrangements were at once made for him to go to a relative of his, living up at Litton, a village a few miles up 'the Dales' - whose name was Gill, a shoemaker - under pretence of his not being well, and needing a change. Jack was willing to go, forever since the Grass Wood tragedy, and the midnight removal of the dead, he had been in a state of great mental torture and bodily fear, and to go anywhere from Grassington he imagined would bring relief. In this, however, he was mistaken, for he felt as uneasy at Litton as he ever had done at Grassington. The voice of conscience was as loud as ever - his days were as comfortless and his nights are sleepless as ever. He not infrequently left the haunts of men to ramble alone in upper Litton Dale, or on the moorlands above to brood in solitude over the fearful events of the past few weeks, as he felt at times so utterly miserable. Conscience should have forced him to make a disclosure of the terrible secret which Tom Lee had lodged in his mind; but the unaccountable fear he had of Tom's vengeance, kept the secret bolted and barred there. It was in one of these rambles that he had met with Betty Knowle, and in the distraction of his mind had given hints that something dreadful preyed upon his mind, but however she pressed him to tell her the cause of his uneasiness, the threatening form of Tom Lee prevented him, and he hurried away from her bearing his heavy burden with him, into the gloomy glen or bleak moorland scene.

Tom having been remanded for a week, the case was heard at Skipton, but notwithstanding all the efforts which old Tobias Sedgwick made to come out at the truth, he found himself unable to bring sufficient evidence to convict. Betty Knowle repeated the conversation she had held with Jack Sharp before the bench, but when Jack was brought into court, though he acknowledged having seen her and talked with her on the day in question, he stoutly denied having said anything - either to implicate himself or anyone else in the matter before the court, consequently the evidence again broke down, and Tom was a second time acquitted. During the investigation Tom seemed somewhat perturbed up to the time when Jack was examined, but on hearing what Jack had to say, he immediately felt relieved, and assumed his usual cold and defiant look, and on leaving the court began to talk rather freely to those around him about insulted innocence, and that perhaps folks would be satisfied in a while, as he scornfully expressed himself, of his being clear, "of that lot, anyhow."

"Thou sets a good face on it, howsomever, Tom," cried out Anthony Edmondson, one of the bystanders.

"Aye," said Tom, with a smile of triumph, "cannot any man set a good face on a thing that he's clear of," and he made his way down Castle Hill, leaving the large crowd that had assembled, to form what opinions they liked on the matter.

"Dunnot flap thy wings so much," shouted after him a woman on the outskirts of the crowd, whose dress and general appearance indicated her migratory habits of life, "maybe thou'll be losing a feather or two if thou does. The time will come when thou will fly high and dry enough."

It was Betty Knowle, the pot-hawker.

CHAPTER VIII   DUST TO DUST – ASHES TO ASHES

In one of the chambers of the Parsonage at Linton a rush-light dimly burned, which, aided by the flickering flames of a fire of logs, gave indistinctly to view the outline of various objects in the room. It had every appearance of a study, for on one side of it stood an oaken bookcase, which contained, for the period, a goodly collection of books consisting for the greater part of classical literature. Sitting in a crimson-coloured open chair was a man who appeared to be about fifty years of age. He had a fine intellectual face, bright restless eyes, but the general expression of his features presented that cynical aspect which plainly told of his being a thorough disciple of Diogenes - his compressed lips denoted to the most casual observer that he had a will of his own, and that having once formed an opinion he dare freely express it and hold it against all comers. He appeared as if the world had not gone well with him -that his pathway through it had not been strewn with flowers, and that he felt little obliged to anyone in it for any favours he had ever received - he appeared to be a disappointed man. On the table at his elbow lay open one of the works of Horace. He had just been reading one of that author's bitterest satires, and in this he frequently found hypochondriacal pleasure. He sat for some time steadfastly gazing into the fire apparently lost in the thoughts which had been started in his mind by reading the satire, but at length reaching out his hand to a small bell on the table he rang it, when it was immediately answered by an attendant whose principal duty was to read to him Latin and Greek.

"I say, Philip," said he, addressing his attendant on entering the room, "I have just been reading Horace's first satire again: it's as good as ever - it's capital, but there's precious little chance of getting rich at Linton, Philip - to think of hoarding wealth here," and he made the chamber ring again with a loud, sarcastic laugh, "I wish with all my heart" – continued he, "that Lord King, the Chancellor, who graciously, ha, ha, presented me with the mediety of the rectory of Linton had been forced to come here among these 'baptised brutes' of parishioners himself, and live all his days on their vile oatcake and porridge."

"Yes, yes, Mr Smith," meekly observed the attendant, who appeared to be the ninety-ninth cousin of Dominie Sampson, of Scotch celebrity, and who always spoke in a slow, deliberate, and pedantic style, "but to an unambitious mind, no doubt you will be prepared to allow, such a living as that of Linton, even among these 'baptised brutes' as you are pleased to term them, is not to be despised. Would that providence would so kindly smile upon me, your humble servant, as to place me in such a liv____."

"What do you mean Sir, what do you mean?" broke in the irascible Mr. Smith, "it is for this that I took you, a half-starved classical scholar as you called yourself, under my protection and shared my dry crust with you? And now you would take the crust altogether out of my mouth. I say it is worse than being banished to Patmos, being sent into this wild district among its uncouth Hottentots, and if my Lord the Earl of Hardwicke had proved the friend he once professed to be to, I should not have remained in this Siberia."

"Compose yourself, compose yourself, my dear sir. Do not for a moment think that in the remark I made I intended to insinuate that - hem -"

"I care nothing about what you did or did not insinuate," again cried out the Rev. Benjamin Smith in a great passion, a state of mind to which he always got when thinking of the shabby way in which he imagined himself to have been treated by the Lord Chancellor who had presented him with his living, "but I wish the whole parish-living and all that goes with it were at the bottom of the Baltic – there," and putting his hands on his knees and leaning forward, he stared his attendant out of all propriety, challenging in his words a reply to his remarks - if the poor attendant dare to make one. No reply was made, however, and the rector, being just in a state of mind for enjoying a little of Horace, he ordered his attendant to read Epistle VIII, being as suitable a one as he could think of. While the attendant was reading, the reverend gentleman proceeded to undress, and going to a recess on one side of the bedroom-chamber in which stood a bed, he laid himself down and listened to the soothing murmur of the reader's voice. After having read for a considerable time the attendant broke off his reading and said, "I suppose, Mr. Smith, that you are not forgetting the fact - hem - that the funeral of Dr Petty takes place here precisely at eleven o'clock tomorrow, and that – hem - it is the wish of – hem – his relict that you should yourself officiate on this important occasion."

"Ah, yes, poor Petty," soliloquized the rector, raising himself to a sitting posture. "It's a pity both for him and his family. He was the only one with whom I had anything in common – I have had many an hour of real intellectual pleasure with him, but he has gone. And how? Mine has been a rough journey through life, but I hope it's end will not be like thine, Petty. Tom Lee must have been connected with that deed, and Tom Lee must and will suffer for it yet. Ah, well, I'm like the aged thorn tree on the heath above, branch after branch of worldly good is being blown off by this ruthless blasts that sweep across the desert worlds of life – well, what care I – the end will come, but Petty, thine is the unfortunate one."

So saying, he ordered his attendant to proceed with his reading, which he continued to do, until the Rev.

Benjamin Smith, rector of Linton, leaving the companionship of Horace and forgetting all the grievances connected with his poor living and Linton, went off on one of his accustomed excursions into the realms of Morpheus. Such was the habit of the eccentric gentleman, four or five times a week when his attendant after having read him to sleep would retire to his own rest.

The morrow came. It was one of those silent wintry days that appear so dreary and dead to those who are accustomed to the activities and bustles of town life. A snowstorm had continued for some days, and every object in nature was covered with sparkling crystals. Farmsteads and cottages scattered on the hillsides or in the vales appeared more than usually isolated, and in the distance scarcely distinguishable from their surroundings. In the village of Linton there were no signs of life excepting here and there a curl of blue smoke ascending silently into the morning gloaming, or a herdsman or two cutting their way to the mistal to attend to the cattle. The trees in the orchard or by the side of the town's gate, as it was called, were feathered with snow, and presented the most beautiful glimpses of fairy-land imaginable. The stream, which flowed right through the centre of the village and under the walls of the hospital - a charitable institution, founded by Richard Fontaine Esquire, (a native of the place who had acquired a large fortune in London), for the maintenance of six poor men or women of the parish - ran merrily along, toiling and smoking among the somewhat large stones lying here and there in its bed and ice-covered sedgy banks. Its voice, and the voice of the church bell which came mournfully across the valley later on in the day, telling of the approach of the funeral cortege from Burnsall, where the only sounds that broke the deep silence that reigned over the scene.

Soon after the commencement of the tolling of the bell, the Rev. B. Smith, followed by his attendant Philip, surpliced and otherwise prepared to perform the solemn rites of the church for the dead, issued from the parsonage and bent his steps in the direction of the church, which stood in the solitary situation on the south bank of the Wharfe, for the equal accommodation of the different townships which comprised the parish. Originally it was a low Norman building with a nave, single choir and north aisle only, but in the reign of Henry VIII, it underwent a thorough repair, and was greatly enlarged. Towards this sacred edifice the mortal remains of Dr Petty were being slowly borne by a friendly few of Wharfedale's sturdy honest yeoman, followed by the weeping widow with her children and relatives. Having borne the coffin near to one of the stalls adjoining the choir, the lattice work of which was adorned with paper garlands carried at the funerals of young unmarried women (as was the custom in most of the churches in Wharfedale), inscribed with the name and age of the deceased, and placed it in the centre of the aisle, the rector entered his stall, and slowly and solemnly commenced reading the beautiful service for the dead. Stormy as was the day, a great many of the inhabitants of the surrounding villages had assembled to witness the mournful ceremony, some from common curiosity, but by far the greater number from deep feelings of sympathy for the bereaved widow and deep respect for the deceased. The doctor had been a cheerful man, with a kind word for everyone and had won the esteem of all around him. His benevolence too had been tasted by many in indigent and afflicted circumstances. Many hearts had often been cheered and sufferings mitigated by his kindly and opportune aid, and his loss would consequently be deeply felt. The solemn words of the rector and the bitter sobs of the widow, distinctly heard in the reigning stillness that pervaded the lonely church, brought a tear to many an eye unused to weeping. Among those present none felt so keenly, perhaps, the mournfulness of the scene as Dick Linton, down whose manly cheeks at one time ran tears of genuine sorrow for the dead and commiseration for the living, tears which he felt did his heart good. Anon a fierce expression would pass over his countenance indicative of the dissatisfaction he felt at the result of the inquest and examination before the magistrates of Tom Lee, the man whom he felt was the cause of the distress he witnessed. The service being over, the body was born to its last resting-place to await the awful trumpet blast that would awaken it to its final and everlasting destiny.

And earthly was the sound which preceded from the grave as the mould looked upon the coffin, accompanied by the solemn words, "dust to dust, ashes to ashes," pronounced by the rector over the departed one. For a considerable time after the disappearance of the rector, as well as of a large number of the lookers-on, the widow stood by the grave of him whom in life she loved so well, looking into it with a broken heart, as if she would fain lay herself down by his side and be at rest; but at last yielding to the entreaties of her friends around, she left the place wailing her last, like Rachel of olden times, and could not be comforted.

"Anthony, excuse me for saying so, but it's like driving a dagger into my heart it is, to see that woman's suffering," said Dick Linton, addressing Anthony Hodgson as they stood near to the church porch watching the widow's retreating form. "My heart's been as tender as a chickens for this last hour; I'm sure I never saw such trouble afore, one minute I've been crying like a child, and next I've been so mad that I couldn't bide to think that he that caused it all should slip the gallows that he so richly deserves, as it seems he has done."

"Do not speak so loud, Dick," said Anthony, "and have patience; I've no doubt that things all right their selves in the long run."

"Well, I've heard them talk about ways of providence being inscrutable, I think that's what they call it, and I guess they mean by that, that they cannot be read; now, if this isn't a case of that sort, I never knew one; patience! Mine were never tried so much afore!"

"Spin it out, Dick, "ratch your patience out," said a masculine-looking woman who stood near and had overheard their conversation, "I've closely watched things in my time and I know "a B from a bull's foot", as much maybe as any a person, and I can tell you this, that the saddle generally gets put on to th' right back." Him that's been the cause of that man coming here," continued she, pointing to the doctor's grave which was being rapidly filled, will never die in his bed, a voice from that grave will be heard up th' Dales till justice has done its work in th' matter, never fear," And Betty Knowle, for it was she, left the graveyard with a tear-bedewed cheek, and with an eye whose prophetic fire, as she uttered her last words, disposed Dick Linton, more than a hundred homilies would have done, to exercise his patience under the tome that, things would right themselves in the end. Soon after, the solitary churchyard contained none but its dead.

In a few weeks after the funeral of Dr Petty, his widow having made arrangements with Mr Diddlegan to succeed to her late husband's practise, left the scene of her sorrow, and went with her children some distance away to reside with a near relative. Such was the strength of her love for her departed husband, however, that the change of scene brought not back her wanted cheerfulness, alleviated not her sorrow, she continually brooded over the mystery of his yet unaccounted for death, and, beyond attending to the welfare of her children, she paid no attention to what was passing in that little world around her. She lived in the deepest collusion the remainder of her days; but she lived long enough to see the mystery solved.

CHAPTER IX   THE COCK FIGHT

Gentle reader, it is now about three years since the period at which our last chapter concluded, and we need not tell you what a number and variety of changes may and do take place in that length of time. Some by a sudden unfavourable turn of the wheel of fortune may be raised from a state of indigent to one of comparative affluence - others may be hurled from a lofty eminence of wealth and pride, towards which they may have been struggling through a lifetime of self-denial and industry, into circumstances of abject poverty. Some who have enjoyed years of uninterrupted health may find their health shattered, and thus the keystone of the arch of all their happiness removed, or fallen into ruins; or those who may have passed through a long course of bitter afflictions may suddenly find themselves restored to the enjoyment of hope-inspiring health, and their freed spirits ready, with all the elasticity of youth, to bound away again into all the duties of pleasure and life. But how many may have passed the dark frontiers of the invisible world, 'doffed their mortal coil' and entered upon their everlasting destiny. Among these our mutual friend, old Anthony Hodgson, is numbered. After the funeral of Dr Petty, the desire to see the mystery of the doctor's death being cleared up grew stronger and stronger, and in his last days, next to the knowledge of his own spirits safety in taking its flight into the unknown, nothing could have given him greater satisfaction then with the intelligence that justice had at length laid hold of those who had taken the doctor's life. This, however, was not to be. Nevertheless, he held the opinion to the last that whoever they were, they would be found out, and though he shrunk from naming those he suspected, he would frequently say, "maybe Dick Linton's words will come true yet," and so it proved so sooner than the perpetrator of the deed expected.

We now travel to the hamlet of Lytton. The village boasts one public house, the proprietor of which is a blacksmith, one Christopher Mytton, or Kitty Mytton, as he was usually called. The village was now in full swing. How the young lads and lasses are enjoying themselves to be sure, in dancing and romping upon the green sward. Would that all the enjoyments of the feast were so innocent; let us go to the top end of the village, and a different sense will be witnessed. A large number of persons surrounded a partly natural and partly artificial hollow, in a greatly excited state. Some were shouting at the top of their voices and some were cursing most bitterly. Every variety of fiendish expression sat up on their countenances, as they all eagerly gazed into the hollow, watching most intently what was going on there. It was a cockpit. Lytton was notorious throughout Craven for its cock-fighting propensities, and on this day no fewer than sixteen birds had been entered to fight, seven encounters had already taken place, and the last for the day was then just commencing. Each bird was closely cropped about the head, and had steel heels tied to its feet with which to deal destruction to its antagonist. Immediate backers of each cock minutely examined the opposing one to see that there was no trickery. They put the cock's head into their mouths, and carefully turned up every feather to see if anything had been put on by which to poison and otherwise disable either of them for continuing the fight. Having found everything to their satisfaction in this respect and arranged all of the preliminaries, the battle began - the birds themselves being apparently as eager for the fray as any of their backers. As the fight preceded, the excitement became more and more intense as fortune appeared to favour either one or the other, for the greatest amount of money was at stake than at any other time during that day. Each bird came warily to the scratch, and seemed to look to take all the advantages that turned up in its favour as much as the most practised and scientific pugilist that ever entered the prize-ring. They fiercely darted at each other's heads and seized it if possible and held it as long as they could, then leaving each other for a short space, would spring at each other again, and with the steel weapon strapped to their heels would try to clinch the head and give the death blow, by driving the steel through the other's neck. Long and fiercely did they fight; they were the best matched pair that had been set against each other during the whole day. They fought till each head seemed to be one mass of bloody pulp, and each had lost an eye, but gradually they became weaker and weaker, and seizing each other's heads they would tenaciously hold on even when they had not strength left to stand. Thus would they lie side by side for a considerable time. The beholders thinking at times that they were both dead, only for them to jump up and reel and stagger towards each other apparently determined to fight to the death. The site was disgusting - but not to them whose heart and soul were wrapped up in the contest, and who were so deeply interested in the result.

"Three to one on the Grassington cock," some shouted out at the top of their voices, the chances of success appearing for the moment to be in its favour.

"Six to one on the Lytton cock, Lytton forever," vociferously shouted the lads of the village, who could not bear the idea of the laurels being borne away from the place. At last the battle came to a close, the Lytton bird making a final effort for victory. He flapped his wings and sprang fiercely at his opponent, raising himself on the ground he concentrated all his remaining power into his heel, and struck the steel through his antagonist's head, who fell dead, bringing down his victor with him to the ground, as it was some time before he could extradite the steel from the head of his fallen foe. This done, in a short time, he got up, placed his feet up on the neck of the dead bird, flapped his wings once more, and very feebly made an attempt to crow his victory, but could only raise two or three notes, and he likewise fell down dead in the arena of strife. Of course, the Lytton cock was declared the victor. Some of the other party, however, contended that as both birds were dead neither was the winner. The dispute ran high, the Lytton boys maintaining that as their cock came up again to the scratch after the other was dead he had won the battle and last stakes should be paid. This was loudly protested against, and by none so much as the owner of the defeated cock, a tall sinewy individual, who brought himself into a perfect rage at having lost his pet bird he declared with dreadful imprecations that he would not pay over the money that the Lyttoners demanded, and he should like to know which of them would make him.

"Well, the money's just here, I'se take it from ye, Tom," said another powerful looking fellow in a taunting tone. "No! You mustn't think of having all your own way here, I'll just mind thee that thee are not at Grassington now. Pay thy brass like a man."

"I'll see thee fat first, fed wi' chips, ye blustering fool," returned the first speaker, "an' if thou thanks thou can make Tom Lee pay what he hasn't a mind to - well try, that's all."

"Thou cursed thief," retorted the enraged Kitty Lytton, for it was he, "I'll not only try but I shall do it, and take that for a beginning," continued he, at the same time fetching Tom a blow between his eyes which levelled him to the earth. Tom, however, speedily sprang to his feet and closed with his well-matched opponent before anyone could interfere to stop the fight. For a short time they grappled with each other, both exerting all their power to throw his opponent. At last, with purple faces and extended eyes, they both fell, Tom Lee being the upmost, but, being near the edge of the declivity sloping down to the banks of the River Skirfare, then began a general engagement; sods and stones and everything they could lay their hands on were thrown at each other. Before they could join issue again the partisans on both sides, who all the time had been bawling and shouting, making the valley ring again with their unearthly commotions, and giving each other desperate blows, rushed between them to separate them. At length the Lyttoners became the victors, driving every one of their opponents out of the valley. Loud rose the shouts of victory as the combatants returned with their scars to the village, accompanied by a fair number of its inhabitants who had been excited and alighted spectators of the melee. Among these none had been more delighted than our old acquaintance, Betty Knowle.

Betty Knowle was just entering the village, leading a donkey by the head, behind which was a small rustic cart loaded with crockery ware (that being the kind of merchandise in which the gypsy-like looking woman dealt, and by which she earned a precarious living), when Tom Lee and Kitty Mitton began their fight.

"Well done, Kitty," shouted she as they neared the village, "I've not sold a single pot this day, but it's done my old heart good to see yon rascal Tom Lee beaten for once. He's a gallows looking thief, but the fate of his cock this day will be his own afore long - see if it isn't."

Kitty Mytton, whose face was covered with blood, though he was less hurt than he appeared to be, replied "Whether he comes to the gallows or not he shan't come here with his bluster and wind while I live at Lytton."

While a few of the leading men in the contest repaired to the inn to fight the battle over again with their tongues, the rest took themselves to the various sports and pastimes that were going on. The greatest hilarity prevailed until a late hour when one group after another, according to the distance they had to go, departed from the village in different directions to their homes, well pleased with their afternoon's enjoyment. At length, after most of the villagers having retired to rest, nothing was heard save the song of the Skirfare as the water merrily ran down the valley.

Meanwhile, Betty Knowle and Kitty Mytton continued their conversation from earlier, and brought it to the following conclusion,

"Tom'll be hanged, assure as he's been beaten today," said Kitty to Betty Knowle.

"What makes ye speak as if ye were so sure about it?" asked Kitty.

"Because I've seen Jack Sharp again," replied Betty, "and he seems nearly out of his mind when Tom Lee is named to him - he seems to be in mortal fear. I saw this and threatened and coaxed him till at last he did all but confess that Tom did the deed."

"Well, said Kitty, "I'se have to go to York before long about this affair and then summat will turn up, but, I say, Betty, keep ye tongue still, or else you'll spoil it all."

"Oh, trust me, Kitty," said Betty, as she left the room to go to her lodgings over the brewhouse, "I wouldn't spoil it for the world." She left Kitty to clear the house of his customers. Soon the villagers were all wrapped in sleep, and the village itself in silence and darkness, only revealed by the dim light of the stars.

CHAPTER X   IMPOSITION OFFERED

Be pleased, reader, to step this way, will you? We are entering one of the Grassington lead mines. Stumble not and follow on without fear; this lamp will give us a little light. It seems to be a new opening - keep out of that little run of water to the right.

There is a solitary miner, sat moodily at work; it was the sound of his pick that we heard just now. His name is John Sunter, who about half a year ago came from Greenhow-Hill with his family and settled at Grassington. His object in coming was to try his luck in mining, indeed his hand has cut the passage we have come along. Month after month as he perseveringly laboured in this arduous undertaking in the hope of being repaid for his toil, and bettering the condition of his family.

After his day's work he throws his tattered coat over his shoulders, after having put a precious bit of ore into one of his pockets and seizing the nearly burnt-out candle, he makes his way out and proceeds towards the village below. Entering the main streets he meets one of those, above all others, excepting his wife, he is most glad to meet, in his now cheerful, mood of mind. It is none other than Kitty Mytton.

"What, John, are ye giving up work so soon?" asked Kitty, "an' looking so pleased too. What is up?"

Kitty Mytton had proved himself to be one of John Sunter's best friends. For some considerable time, Tom Lee had sharpened John Sunter's mining tools, and continued to do so while there was a prospect of being paid, and even for some time after, but Sunter's continued ill luck caused him to close the account. Kitty Mytton hearing of this generously offered to do the work for him. It was this generous act which made John Sunter's heart feel so glad when he met Kitty. For a moment or two he could not reply to Kitty's question, but pulling him by his jacket lap to a quiet corner a short distance from the road he at length said,

"Kitty, I have found it, but Kitty don't say a word to anybody, I'm trying to throttle my joy."

In carrying out his mining he had braved the pangs of gnawing hunger for hundreds of hours.

"What think ye, John, if we go down to the Blue Anchor, and talk things over a bit? Tom Lee will not have come out of th' smithy yet, maybe, and we can be to ourselves a bit."

To this John agreed, and as they went down he eagerly told Kitty all about his accidentally lighting upon a bed of ore, just as he was giving the job up for the day. Kitty was delighted but advised him to keep his tongue still about it. When they got to the Blue Anchor, however, small chance was there to talk matters fully over as they intended, for who should be there but our old friend Dick Linton, and Luke Splitcurran, the village grocer - a man whose only object in life was to see how little money he could live on every day he did live, and how much money he could save every day. He was reputed to be very wealthy. He had supplied John Sunter with goods for which Sunter was unable to pay, and consequently John owed him a rather heavy sum of money. It appeared that Dick Linton had likewise owed him a trifle for some time.

There was a dispute between the men over the amount owed and Luke Splitcurran banged an account down on the table.

"I've heard him name that amount o' money many a time and I swear it in any court in England," broke in

Dick Linton, giving the table a hearty thump at the same time, to add force to what he had said.

"An' I'll sweat that Luke never said any other sum but eleven pounds ten, an' Jack Sharpe'll swear the same," defiantly set Tom Lee, just then entering the room, having heard all the dispute going on behind the door. Tom had his reasons for entering into the dispute; he was grieved to his heart that Sunter had gone to Kitty Mytton to have his tools sharpened, even when he himself had refused to do the work from a fear of never being paid; he, like the grocer, wished to see the miner fast; not that Sunter had ever done him any harm, but from a wanton, devilish whim to injure others, which, alas, too many, under similar circumstances, indulged in. Besides, Tom hated Dick Linton, and in opposing him would do or swear anything, right or wrong.

"Why, what's time to do with it, you great pot mouth, thou will swear that black's white anytime and anywhere - for a penny," shouted Dick to Lee, for the very sight of Tom always raised his bile.

"Why," said Tom, "if Luke'll take the case to York I'll back him through thick and thin; you're not going to have things your own way I can tell you that!"

"I should like no better fun, then the case going there," broke in Kitty Mytton, "ye shall be matched for once."

"Well, ye shall have th' chance to match us then. For as sure as I'm a living man it shall go to York," said the grocer, at the same time jumping up from his chair and fixing his eyes on Kitty, he continued, "Ye're a big man up at Lytton, but ye mustn't come it down here - I'll crop your beard for ye, see if I don't." And the grocer left the room in a towering passion.

Dick, standing with a pint pot in his hand, just ready to swipe off the remainder of its contents, at the same time eyeing Tom Lee, said, "I say. Tom and me will have to try which one can swear hardest this time, but before I go, I'll give thee a toast - may all that go to York return home again, alive and well."

Before Tom could reply all three had gone, and he was left to chew the bitter cud of reflection suggested by the sly insinuation couched in the last remark Dick Linton made. For some time after this both sides were anxiously preparing for appearing at York, there to have the case tried; and it was to this state of things to which Kitty Mytton had alluded at the close of the last conversation with Betty Knowle.

CHAPTER XI   A RIDE TO YORK

To York the case had therefore to go to be tried. All was in readiness, the witnesses on both sides were all secured, and had received notice to answer to their names in the Court of Justice, to be held at the forthcoming summer assize. At length the day of trial came and arrangements were made for the parties interested in the matter to set off early in the morning of the day previous, so as to be in readiness when the case came on.

Dick again asked Kitty to what he referred to in the hint he had thrown out earlier, "Why, see thee, Dick, it's just this. I've an idea that Tom Lee will never come home again – he's gettin' to the length of his tether."

"Hurrah, does thou think so?" shouted Dick, in ecstasy, "but," continued he, "As thou any solid ground for thy idea, 'cause of thou has, we're going to be rid of that regular pest."

"I've grounds enough, I'm afraid," answered Kitty, in a sad tone.

And here Kitty preceded to relate to Dick all that Jack Sharp, Tom's apprentice, had divulged to Betty Knowle; and that if Jack could be insured of his safety he would make a clean breast of it and that at York the apprentice would be in a great measure to be out of the clutches of Tom - that if Tom would be quiet he did not wish to take any mean advantage of him, but if not, why, he would have to take the consequences.

And so did they talk, until they came to a perfect understanding as to their plan of proceedings upon their arrival at York. Having arranged that they, together with John Sunter, would start off early the following morning, Dick left Lytton for home.

By four o'clock the following morning our trio, each on horseback, were leisurely ascending the hillside above Grassington towards the extensive moorlands across which lay their way to the fine valley of the Nidd.

As they crossed over the bridge, the first inn they came at, just at the bottom of the hill leading up to the town in one direction, and up to the ancient castle was the 'World's End Inn'; on the opposite side of the river were the celebrated Dropping Wells.

"Let's go in and let the horses have summat to eat," said Kitty, and he led the way to the stables. No sooner had they got in and Dick turned round and whispered to Kitty, "There's Tom Lee here – see thee! That's his grey pony in the far yonder stall. Should we still stop here now then?"

"Aye, for sure," said Kitty, "Is Tom any better than we are?"

"No, no, "answered Dick, "I thought there might be a row among us, that's all."

They soon after entered the house; and the first sound they heard was Tom Lee's voice, as he loudly berated poor Jack Sharp for having lost a five-shilling piece on the road. Indeed, the apprentice had a miserable life of it with Tom, and with himself as well. The idea of going to York was anything but palatable to him - he connected it with the idea of something dreadful. He was so nervous with the weight of guilt on his conscience that he knew not what he was doing one half of the time; besides, he felt himself to be so much in the power of Tom that, well knowing his desperate character, he did not consider his life to be worth the moments purchased, and what was worse for himself, he had the fixed idea that there was no means of escape – he was the bird, Tom was the basilisk.

"My heart fair works for you, lad," said Dick to his companions, as Tom's thundering, threatening, bullying tones from one of the other rooms ever and anon reached them.

"Let's keep away from him as long as we can, we shall come to loggerheads before we get home," said Kitty.

However, whilst the last word was on his lips, a crash, as of a chair being broken, reached their ears, accompanied with a cry from Jack Sharp, and scream from Tom's wife.

"I can stand it no longer," cried Dick Linton, springing to his feet and rushing into the other room, where he found Jack Sharp with a stream of blood flowing from his nose. Tom's fist up raised to inflict another blow, and Tom's wife deprecatingly raising her arms between them to prevent another blow.

Kitty shouted, giving the table a vigorous thump, "Thou's getting to the end of thy tether every mile thou gets nearer to York, thou's gets nearer thy long deserved doom. In point of law, I believe the lad belongs to thee, as thy apprentice, but thou uses him so cruelly that it shall be as Dick has said; and if thou doesn't like it, when thou gets home again, thou can go to the law, and mend thyself if thou can."

Tom prepared for desperate measures by seeking the poker, but his wife and the landlord here interfered to prevent hostilities. Tom was not at all sorry at losing Jack to the trio, as he had been a source of annoyance to Tom ever since they left Grassington, and the latter declared he would not have the neighbourhood raised up by Tom; before he would, he would give him into the hands of the police, as already a number of persons had gathered around the door. Jack was only too pleased at the turn things had taken, and soon after was enjoying a hearty meal with his deliverers. Tom's heart was now a volcano but he soothed himself with the thought that the time would come when he could pull out the burning lava of his pent-up wrath, and consume those who now triumphed over him.

In all that had taken place, both Kitty and Dick had an object in view, which not only embraced Jack's complete deliverance from Tom, but to prove the guilt of Tom in the murder of Dr. Petty. This object they did not communicate even to John Sunter, so much afraid were they of not succeeding in the plans which they had laid down. This was nothing more than to get Jack so far intoxicated and unguarded as to confess the whole thing to them - to get him to turn King's evidence and bring Tom to justice. They determined, therefore, having succeeded so far in their plot as to get Jack into their hands, that they would carry out the rest when they arrived at York that night.

In about an hour after the altercation with Tom, that person and party set out for York. Not deeming it prudent to follow till Tom had got a good start of them, so as to prevent another collision with him, our party sat a considerable time after dinner, plying Jack with liquor and winning his confidence as gradually and unsuspectingly as they could.

After having done this as far as they thought prudent before they got to York they set out for the scene of their next day's action. After a rather wearisome ride, they arrived safely in the ancient northern metropolis. They put up at a quiet inn, in a quiet street, by the side of a quiet church.

CHAPTER XII   PROVEN AT LAST

Gloomy was the wind, bitter and vindictive the feelings of Tom Lee when he himself arrived at York. He was morose and unapproachable even to his wife. In vain did she endeavour to assuage his pent-up wrath, all the more fiercely burning in his heart's core because it was pent-up. In vain did she whisper hopes into the ear of a successful issue of the pending trial, and that when he returned to Wharfedale, where Dick Linton and Kitty Mytton and, for their unpleasant interference with him at Knaresborough. The grasping, covetous, overreaching old grocer, Luke Splitcurran, also found that he had allied himself to a bad cause, with anything but a pleasant partner. Tom had thoughts and feelings of which neither his wife nor the grocer had any idea. For some time he had mistrusted Jack Sharp – Lee had got it into his head that either Jack had divulged some part of the dreadful secret which he held, or that he would be doing so soon, partly pressed by the noise of a guilty conscience and partly by those who around him, whom Lee felt, would only be too glad to poke their fingers into the secret.

Since Jack had got into the hands of the two persons whom Lee feared most, he became more and more under easy, under the apprehension that his secret by some means or other would ooze out. Lee felt that in the case of Splitcurran v Sunter, he was going deliberately to swear falsely, and drag Jack into the same sin just to gratify his personal feelings of revenge, not so much against Sunter as against the miner's witnesses; but he felt, as thousands had felt before – the more he hated and tried to injure others, the more powerless he became to accomplish his black designs – arising not only from a consciousness of his own hellish motives and guilty deeds, but from the all-controlling influence of the presentiment of the coming retribution hanging over him like a heavy, smothering pall, which made him shrink inside himself – and made a perfect coward of him. Tom's proud, strong spirit began to bend under the thick gathering apprehensive thoughts and feelings which pressed upon his distracted brain. Whatever was the upstroke of the gathering events he determined to brave them, and face the worst that might happen.

In the quiet inn, in the quiet street, by the quiet church, Dick Linton and Kitty Mytton were quietly enjoying themselves. Living the most exact of lives, and too fond perhaps of partaking of the forbidden fruit which grew in such tempting profusion on both sides of the pathway along which they were called to pass through this world, yet the laws of their country had no terrors for them. Tom Lee was miserable under the most direful apprehensions of coming ills; they at least could enjoy their pipe and drop of beer in comparative peace. Such is the difference between guilt and innocence. Before retiring to bed on the night of their arrival at York they plied Jack Sharp not only with beer but with all the persuasive kindness which their rough natures could command to extort from him the secret they felt sure he possessed. They got a partial confession, but nothing on which they could base their intended operations.

Though Jack felt more secure from Tom Lee than he ever had done since the death of Dr Petty, he could not wholly divest himself of the great fear of Tom, and hence, hitherto he had not made a full confession. The fear of self-implication and the dreadful punishment, consequent upon such proved implication, likewise deterred him from confessing, but Dick and Kitty having found out his weak point, resolved after the trial on the following day to ply him again and convince Jack that, as he had ruthlessly been dragged into the matter by Tom Lee against his own wish and free will, he, by turning King's evidence, would be pardoned, if he brought the real perpetrator of the deed to justice.

In the afternoon of the following day, the case came on for trial, into the particulars of which it would be a needless task to enter, further than saying that from the improbable claim of the grocer upon John Sunter, considering the comparatively short time in which such a heavy score was run up by a man of such well known economical habits as the miner, together with the contradictory evidence given by Tom Lee and Jack Sharp, the false witnesses which old Luke Splitcurran had brought into court as his supporters, the jury was not long in coming to a verdict in favour of the defendant – the grocer having to pay all the expenses for his trouble. The result of this decision going through Luke's pocket, found its way into his covetous heart, and then spread throughout his whole frame in a tornado of passion. To lose money was the greatest evil that could befall Luke Splitcurran, and Tom in turn got soundly rated by the excited grocer. Tom then flew at his wife, expending part of his wrath upon her. Everything was out of joint. He took to drinking, but that only made him more desperate, and, losing the little cunning reason that had hitherto partially controlled him, he set out late at night to Jack Sharp's lodgings, intending to give him and his new masters the full benefit of his burning ire.

No sooner was the trial over than John Sunter, accompanied by his solicitor and witnesses, together with Jack Sharp, returned to their lodgings in the quiet inn, all in the very best spirits at the favourable turn things had taken - all except Jack, who had been in a bewildered state of mind ever since they had left Knaresborough – he had scarcely known what to think or say during the trial, and however secure he tried to feel in the company of his present friends, yet the fear of sooner or later tasting the tender mercies of Tom Lee, never left him; indeed the feeling had grown stronger since the termination of the trial.

Dick Linton was in ecstasy over the outcome, and boldly affirmed that it was solely on account of the straightforward way in which he had given evidence. Dick had made up his mind to treat his visit to York and their triumph over the grocer and Tom Lee, as a celebration. He soon began to be boisterously talkative, besieging Jack, so as to set himself up for the accomplishment of his designs against Tom Lee.

At length, what with the kindness of his friends, the quantity of whisky punch he had imbibed, and being fully convinced by the lawyer that no danger whatever would be risked by himself in confessing what he knew of the murder of Dr Petty, Jack Sharp made a full confession of the whole matter.

"Why, we'll be aiders and abettors in this matter if we don't take means at once to bring this Tom Lee to justice," said the lawyer.

"That's true enough," said Dick, "whatever Tom Lee does or does not, we should not be doing our duty to hide this matter from the public." As he spoke they heard the sound of angry voices in the bar room, "I'll eat my knuckles if one of them isn't Tom Lee," said Dick in a loud whisper, leaning over the table. "What's to be done? He's coming this way, whatever the landlord says, an' he's as fresh as a bobbin, my word but there'll be a row now! I say, Jack, come and sit at th' back of me."

But taking advantage of their surprise, and terrified at the idea of meeting Tom, Jack Sharp had crept out of the room, and left the house by the back door. The moment after he left the room Tom Lee entered it. Directly after, the latter beat open the door and stood in the middle of the room, the concentration of malice, hate and revenge. Fixing his eyes upon Kitty, he thundered forth the monosyllable, "Nah!"

Kitty returned his gaze unflinchingly. In in his utterance Tom was frenziedly desperate.

"Where's Jack Sharp?" vociferated Tom.

"He's out of thy clutches, anyway," said Dick, with a sarcastic smile.

"But I'll have him or else have all your lives," shouted Tom, at the same time pulling off his coat and pulling out a large clasp-knife and brandishing it about like a madman. "If ye think that both of ye are a match for me, try it on – I ask ye once more to deliver Jack Sharp up."

"Thou can do as thou likes," shouted Kitty, downright nettled at Tom's murderous preparation for a fight, "he's not here, an' if he were, if thou put a finger on him, thou would pay dearly for it." Seeing Tom about to spring at them, they both sprang to their feet. Kitty, who had prepared for extremities, at the same time drew a pistol from his breast, and, pointing it at Tom continued, "come but a step closer, and thou art a dead man."

The unexpected action staggered Tom considerably - he was like a tiger at bay – foiled again, his rage knew no bounds – he was speechless for a time with hate. At length Lee said, with set teeth and quivering frame, "you're a couple of sneaking thieves and cowards. Mark me! My time will come when I'll settle with ye."

"Never!" shouted Dick.

"Never in this world," shouted Kitty, tremendously excited, "and as for us being thieves, it's a lie. But I'll tell thee what thou art. You're nowt but a rogue, a thief, and a murderer, an' I can prove it, an' will do so before that leaves York!"

"Aye, and I'll make thee prove it," said Tom, as he left the room, now glad to be out of it. For with Kitty's and Jack's absence, the thought like a thunderbolt shot through his heart that Jack must have told – he was completely staggered for a moment or two – he knew not what to do. His first thought was to brave it out, the same as he had done at the inquest – the second was to flee the country at once, and getting safely away, to crack his fingers at Jack's confession, if he had made one, as well as at justice and all its myrmidons. With a view to carry this plan out, he made at once to his lodgings to secure a little money and other necessary things, to take with him. Just as he as he was leaving the inn where he had been staying, an ominous voice broke the stillness of the midnight hour, which so paralysed him that he had not the strength to take a single step in flight.

"That's him, officers!" voiced Mr Paget, the lawyer, and Lee was seized by two officers of justice, who had once marched him away to a place of security, on the grave charge of murdering Dr Petty.

This was no sooner done than Kitty was taken with a regular cold sweat – he had been the means of passing a fellow man over to sure and certain doom. The moment he had done it he wished to undo it, partly out of commiseration for Tom and partly because he thought he had brought himself into a complex fix in bringing the charge of murder against a man, and the most material evidence in the case having fled, for no one knew where Jack Sharp had absconded. All trace of Jack had been lost for some hours; but, thanks to our man of law, he, in conjunction with a few detective officers, succeeded on the following day in bringing back to York the fugitive, Jack Sharp, who had managed to get a considerable way from the city to Liverpool. On again being assured by the lawyers that he need apprehend no danger to himself in the prosecution of Tom, the terrified Jack braced his nerves for the formidable task of confronting his old master and the judge. No time was lost in getting the case ready for court – all of the material was at hand in the shape of evidence and witnesses, which would leave no moral doubt on the mind of anyone as to Tom's guilt, and soon – too soon for Tom Lee -the day of the trial came.

His wife's feelings may be better Imagined than described. The prospect of losing her husband, bad as he was, of her home being broken up, and of her children being reduced to destitution, drove her to distraction, only relieved by the hope that, as when examined before, Tom would have the good fortune of getting off again.

Luke Splitcurran felt so mortified at losing his errand to York and his money as well, that he left for home at the first opportunity that presented itself – although he was secretly gratified, rather than otherwise, at the awful position in which Tom Lee was placed, as his words, to the driver of the conveyance in which he returned home, as they passed through Knaresborough, testified,

"He lost my trial – serve him right if he loses his own. I sould never have come to York but for him."

Different thoughts, however occupied the breast of honest John Sunter as he gazed upon Tom Lee, when he stood in the dock confronting the judge during the trial. The case did not occupy the court very long. The evidence was so conclusive and given in such a telling, convincing manner, under the summing-up of the judge was given in such a terse, plain, and clear way, that the minds of the jury were made-up before they left the court as to the solemn duty they had to perform – no one there could entertain the slightest doubt as to what the verdict would be. During their absence a slight hum of whispered conversation might be heard, which only made the ominous silence that reigned throughout the court more ominous still. Tom Lee seemed to be the most disinterested party present – he foolishly indulged in the hope that after all the verdict would be in his favour, and failing that, he had resolutely made-up his mind to brave the worst. Neither Dick Linton, Kitty Mytton, nor anyone else could experience the slightest gratification of seeing one particle of fear evinced by him. No, no, if he was to die, he would die game.

At last the jury returned into the court. The silence was really oppressive – every face, on which was depicted the most intense anxiety to hear the verdict pronounced, or stretched out in the direction of the foreman. The question was put by the clerk of the court –

"Gentlemen of the jury, how find you, is the prisoner at the bar guilty or not guilty?"

"Guilty, my Lord," was the answer; and the judge assuming the black cap, preceded at once to pronounce sentence. Whilst pronouncing the solemn words a long, loud, piercing shriek rang through the court, alarming everyone, and striking terror through the heart of the now doomed Tom Lee – it was his wife, who, no longer supported by hope, on hearing the dreadful words from the lips of the judge, fell senseless into the arms of those about her, and was borne out of court. The sentence was that the prisoner was to be hung by the neck till he was dead, and his body gibbeted on the spot where the unnatural and cold-blooded deed had been committed. Tom was at once removed to the condemned cell, with an apparently callous indifference to all that was passing around him. Old John Sunter groaned in spirit, and shook his head at Dick Linton, expressive out of the deep pity he felt for Tom's fate, even though he had led a wild, immoral life.

When Tom was left to himself, however, that callous demeanour was thrown off. There is a vast difference in the feelings of a man when he is free to rove anywhere he pleases and is out of reach of the laws of the country, than of a man confined in the last resting place in life, shut up to his own reflections and having the sword of offended justice brandished over his head to take away his life! When by himself, the spirit of the strong man was bowed down, accepting now and then, when he thought of those whom he imagined would be crowing over his downfall. These paroxysms over, he would settle down again with mournful feelings, when he thought of having to leave beautiful Wharfedale. But the die was now cast. He felt he had foolishly chosen to lead an irregular, vicious life; and he felt – oh, how stingingly he felt! – that he must now meet the consequences.

The day before his execution his wife visited his cell. It was a gloomy meeting. He knew he had been the means of gradually leading the wife of his youth from the practise of the principle of honesty, to connive at his nefarious practises; and she was burdened with the thought that she had too readily given way to the temptation. He advised her, on getting back home, to arrange matters as speedily as possible, and remove with the family to some strange place, and endeavour to procure an honest livelihood, and train the children up to a virtuous course of life. Their last parting embrace was touching indeed; she was frantic with grief and clung so strongly to him, that the turnkeys had to use a little gentle force in getting her out of the cell. Tom bowed his head in unutterable trouble, and when alone shed a copious shower of tears, which appeared to relieve his oppressed heart. On the approach of footsteps, however, he removed all traces of sorrow, determined to display no weakness to anyone now that the parting with his wife was over.

The next party who now visited him"were'two turnkeys accompanied by a blacksmith, who had come to measure him for the gibbet irons.

A few minutes before eight o'clock, the following morning, the solemn tones of the death-bell announced that Tom's 'destined hour' had arrived. A large concourse of people had assembled to witness his launch into eternity. Tom mounted the scaffold with a firm step; but, though disdaining to fear man, his lips might have been seen moving, as in prayer to the dread supreme – before whom the mightiest of earth's inhabitants are but as grasshoppers – for that mercy which both the best and worst so greatly need. The bolt was drawn, and Tom Lee expiated his crime with an awful penalty, and had done, here on earth, both with human laws and human vengeance.

On the afternoon of the day after the execution of Tom Lee, the vehicle used for such purposes might have been seen slowly ascending the hill-side from the top end of the valley of the Nidd, leading to the solitary moorland road away in the direction of Greenhow Hill, containing his remains. A short distance before it rode three horsemen who, a few days before, had crossed the same moorland in such good spirits, with such glee and such enjoyment. Far different were their feelings now. Their foe was behind them, dead, their souls were sad at the thought. Very few words passed among them during the mournful journey. Jack Sharp had started on the morning of that day for his native vale. Tom's wife rode behind the corpse, a solitary mourner, almost frantic with grief, but determined to follow the remains of her husband – not to the grave

– that would indeed have been some consolation to her in her deep misery, for she was denied the satisfaction of even burying her dead out of her sight, but to Grassington, where the gibbet was already erected upon which the body was to be suspended, as a warning to evil doers and a terror of crime. The road led by the foot of Caud Stone, an immense piece of rock that jutted out of the hill, and overhung in some places on the highway. On top of this the figure of a woman might have been seen in a sitting posture from a considerable distance. She was attired In a tattered red cloak, the hood of which fell back upon her shoulders, and a faded, shapeless old silk bonnet amply covered her head. Her sunburned, masculine face presented a striking cast of features; it was oval – her mouth puckered with the wrinkles of age, still showed to a great extent strong determination. Her hawk's eyes twinkled from the depths of their setting, seemingly with inward joy. Every feature was rigidly impassive. She seemed to be the weird spirit of the solitary scene. As our travellers reached the point of the road underneath the rock she sat up on, she slowly rose, stretched forth her long, lean arm, and a voice distinctly heard by the passers-by, she cried out –

"Dick Linton, ye remember my sermon in Linton churchyard, on th' day that the doctor was buried. It was a short one. But, look on that body this day, and say wasn't it a true one? I should rejoice this day, but mercy forbid that I should – Betty Knowle knows human nature too well for that."

And Betty Knowle, who had been apprised of the events which had been transpiring at York, disappeared behind the rock, and her retreating form was seen sometime after by Dick Linton on the distant ridge of the moor, just as it dropped out of sight. It was the last he ever saw of Betty, and her last words made a deep and lasting impression upon his mind.

Soon after they passed through the small hamlet of Greenhow Hill, every one of the inhabitants of which were in the town's gate to watch the body pass. Some entertained hard thoughts of Tom's wife in connection with the part she had taken in aiding and abetting her husband in his evil practises, but the greater part commiserated with her regarding her present abject condition, excusing her, due to the consideration of the strong, iron, all-controlling will of Tom forcing her to do what her better nature would have recoiled from.

They reached Grassington at night, and the excitement which prevailed there far exceeded any that they had witnessed at any place on the whole route they had come. Tom's wife was prevailed upon to follow her husband's remains no further, but resign them at once to the fate which justice had decreed; and that very night they were suspended on a gibbet prepared for them -and there they hung, a terror to the whole country. They dropped piecemeal by piecemeal, until at length nothing was left but the bare skeleton of the once notorious Tom Lee. For four years, it is said, that all or part of his bones hung up on that gibbet post and as they dropped they were born off by gipsies and other vagrants who frequented the neighbourhood. The irons, it is also said, were thrown into the Wharfe for a time, and eventually, at the building of Grassington Bridge, they were buried under one of its abutments. The widow following out of the wishes of Tom, expressed in the condemned cell at York, and soon after left the neighbourhood with her family forever.

Jack Sharp went to live with his relative, the shoemaker, and devoted himself to the same business, but ever afterwards was an ailing man, such was the shock his nervous system had received in connection with the unhappy fate of Dr Petty, and the forced part he had had to play in the dark tragedy. Both Kitty Mytton and Dick Linton led better lives ever after, the latter frequently observing both to himself and to others,

"He saw very plainly that it won't do to tamper with any sort of wrongdoing."

THE END

Legend or Fact?

Having read this version of the Tom Lee story, it is fascinating to compare it with the known and recorded facts.

Robertshaw's story was first published in 1862, in *Yorkshire Tales and Legends*, before being edited on three further occasions. Its final printed version appeared as *The Grass Wood Tragedy* in 1907. Almost as intriguing as the tale itself is the improbability that it has, firstly, matured into the definitive and most believed version of events, and secondly, it has become the version upon which all subsequent versions of the story are based. The implausibility of so much of the story simply does not bear scrutiny. For example, how could the writer possibly detail the exact conversations between the many characters, or describe their emotions at any given point in the story?

The improbability that all the necessary witnesses in a minor debt trial conveniently happened to be in York at the same time as Tom Lee, thus miraculously leading to his conviction, is of course ludicrous.

The characters are bizarrely and inconsistently named throughout the story. Whilst Tom Lee, Dr Petty, and

Christopher Mitton are given their correct names (although Dr Petty's first name is never mentioned), many others are not. Dr Diddlegan and Luke Splitcurran are clearly invented, seemingly in the style of Charles Dickens, and many of the others are merely pseudonymous or names derived from real personalities in the story – Dick Linton, Jack Sharp, Jerry Fenton, Betty Knowles, Dame Hodgson, Jim Brown, Peter Dawson, Peter Bentham, Ned Sykes, et al. Tobias Sedgwick, the magistrate from Skipton, is perhaps a conflation of the well-known Sidgwick family from Skipton and Tobias Croft, the rector of Linton from 1750 to 1765.

John Sunter's lawyer, Mr Paget, was a genuine character, however, the real Mr Paget actually practiced law in Skipton between 1840 to 1898. Therefore, he clearly could not have been Sunter's solicitor in 1768.

The story appears to have been dragged out to create a murder mystery, when the culprit is abundantly clear from the outset. Tom Lee was overheard threatening the doctor and moving the corpse. In addition, his reputation preceded him. The only real mystery is why it took the people of Wharfedale two years to convict him.

Whilst the basic facts within the 'Heather Bell' version are correct and corroborated by existing evidence from the time (the body was moved, Tom was tried in

York, his body was gibbeted, etc), much of the remainder of the story seems to be irrelevant detail, wrapped in a Victorian author's intention to instruct us in the dangers of loose morals.

Robertshaw's version seems far more likely to have been based on third and fourth generation handed down local tradition, rather than access to historical documentation. Remember, he is describing a murder which took place a century earlier. Local legend seems to have already muddied the waters. In addition, Robertson, writing around 1860, describes the death of Dr Petty as having taken place 'about 90 years ago', which would place the crime in the early 1770s. We know for a fact that Dr Petty was murdered in 1766.

Some of the locations named in this version are also incorrect. Dr Petty was buried at Linton and not Burnsall. And the Bridge Tavern at Burnsall is surely the Red Lion?

There are also several details which have become unconditionally accepted as fact, of which there is no proof whatsoever. Despite a plaque attesting to this point being clearly displayed in Main Street, Grassington, there is no indication that Tom Lee was ever a blacksmith. Jack Sharp was not Tom Lee's apprentice — there is no proof he ever had one. Dr Petty had also, not been carrying out his medical rounds on the night of his murder; he had been attending a cock-fight.

One fact, almost certainly added for dramatic effect, is that Dr Petty was married with children, and that his wife left the area shortly afterwards. The doctor was a bachelor.

Joseph Robertshaw's version is merely a romanticised novel, loosely based on historic fact, liberally sprinkled with local legend.

Perhaps the fault lies, not with the author, who created a long-lasting, influential, and satisfying piece of entertainment, but with subsequent historians and readers for interpreting rather unconvincing fiction as historical fact.

"Legendary truth is of another nature than historical truth. Legendary truth is invention whose result is reality."

– Victor Hugo

Bibliography and Acknowledgements

Oxford Journal (9 April 1768), *Leeds Intelligencer* (19 July 1768), *Newcastle Courant* (23 July 1768), *Leeds Intelligencer* (26 July 1768), *Stamford Mercury* (28 July 1768), *Manchester Mercury* (2 August 1768), *The Newcastle Weekly Courant* (24 Jul 1784), *Gleanings After Eugene Aram (1836),* by Norrison Scatcherd, *Craven Herald 1853-57* (Articles by Dr James Dixon), *Tom Lee: A Wharfedale Tragedy (1858),* by Heather Bell (Joseph Robertshaw), *Criminal Chronology of York Castle* (1867), by W. Knipe, *Philip Neville of Garriton (1875),* by Rev. Bailey John Harker, *Alston Moor: Its Mine and Its Miners (1890),* by W. Wallace, *The Striding Dales (1929)*, by Halliwell Sutcliffe, *History of Grassington (1979),* by Susan D. Brooks, Tom Lee (1982), by R. Geoffrey Rowley, *Punishments of Former Days (1992)* by Pettifer, Ernest, *Oxford English Dictionary, 3rd Ed.,* Oxford University. *Gibbeting, by Rob Gallagher* (Nov 2008), *The Register of St Mary's Chapel Conistone 1567 – 1812, The Vintage News* (Article 22 Aug 2022), *Manchester Mercury*, *Higher Wharfedale* (1904) by Edmund Bogg, *Yorkshire Gazette* (1901), *Nidderdale* (1863), by William Grainge,

Petyt – Newiss Genelogy, Craven Museum, York Castle Museum, Find My Past, Ancestry.com, The Stripey

Badger Bookshop Grassington, National Library of Medicine, Hebden History Society, The Thoresbury Society, Leeds-List, The UK Paranormal Database.

All the images contained within this book are in the public domain, or their original copyright is not known. Photographs of John Petty's accounts and Dr Petty's saw case appear courtesy of the Craven Museum, Skipton.

The Author

After many years buried in research, Mark Bridgeman released his first book, The River Runs Red, in 2019. The book became an instant success and has been reprinted three times. Further best-selling titles, Blood Beneath Ben Nevis and The Dark Side of the Dales followed in 2020.

Mark's history of an abandoned Scottish community, The Lost Village of Lawers, achieved worldwide success in 2021 when the village became a global news story, resulting in TV appearances on ITV and Channel 5.

In 2022 Mark was nominated for the John Bryne Writing Award as well as appearing on BBC TV and Radio, Heartland FM, Vancouver Radio, and The History Channel.

The Nearly Man, Mark's biography of a little known Scottish war hero turned villain, has been nominated for the prestigious James Tait Black Biography Award and resulted in Mark being asked to guest speak at the prestigious Aberdeen Grammar School.

In 2022 Perthshire's Pound of Flesh become a Waterstones' Book of the Year, voted for by their staff and customers.

Mark has also seen his stories serialised in newspaper form and adapted for Canadian radio.

You can follow @markbridgemanauthor on Facebook, Instagram, X, and Threads or subscribe for updates via www.markbridgemanauthor.co.uk

BRINDLE

BOOKS

Brindle Books Ltd

We hope that you have enjoyed this book. To find out more about Brindle Books Ltd, including news of new releases, please visit our website:

http://www.brindlebooks.co.uk

There is a contact page on the website, should you have any queries, and you can let us know if you would like email updates of news and new releases. We promise that we won't spam you with lots of sales emails, and we will never sell or give your contact details to any third party.

If you purchased this book online, please consider leaving an honest review on the site from which you purchased it. Your feedback is important to us, and may influence future releases from our company.

To view our current releases, please scan the QR code below: